Margarita Sidorenko

All Made of Wool!
Needle Felting

Step-by-Step Instructions and Online Videos.
For Kids 6+ and Beginner Adults

For any questions, comments or suggestions, email us at:
kostyayaroshenkocat@gmail.com

Table of Contents

Needle Felting 4
Tools and Materials 4
Safety Precautions 5

1. Wool Painting 7
2. Appliqué on Clothes and Other Items 12
3. Bracelet 16
4. Earrings 20
5. Needle Felting a Lily Flower 24
6. Felting a Wire-Based Flower 30
7. Owl the Brooch 35
8. Hedgehog the Needle Holder 40
9. Frog 44
10. Snowman the Christmas Tree Ornament 49
11. Snail 54
12. Rabbit 61
13. Dog 70
14. Wire-Based Doll 77
15. Wet-Felted Doll Dress 84

All Videos (Playlist) 92

Needle felting is a very exciting creative process. You can make anything you want out of wool: fashionable jewelry, bags, paintings, cozy clothing and interior items, shoes, charming toys, as well as amazing patterns on fabrics. No special training is required to master this type of handicraft, just some colorful wool, a few tools, and a lot of patience.

In this book, you will learn about the different properties of wool and find detailed instructions on how to make things using various techniques. The book is suitable for beginners. Children from the age of 6–7 and adults of any age will be able to make these items, since they are simple to create. Try it out yourself!

A piece of wool is shaped with the fingers and then pierced many times with a special needle. As a result, the wool fibers bind tightly together, forming an even material. In this way, any shape can be created, just like in sculpture.

Tools and Materials

Wool

Only natural wool is suitable for needle felting, regardless of which animal it came from. The most accessible type is sheep's wool. It consists of thick fibers called guard hairs and soft down fibers. The thinner the wool fiber, the faster it felts and the lighter and softer the finished product will be. During the process, it shrinks significantly (becomes denser), so it is worth stocking up on a large amount of material.

Felting needles

Needles at the bottom have notches that catch the fibers, allowing them to entangle more easily and quickly. For this work, you will need needles of different thicknesses and shapes. **Thin, star-shaped needles** are used to add the finishing touches. The higher the gauge number, the thinner the needle. If you want, for instance, to create fur on the figure, use thin reverse needles.

Brush mats or foam pads

A brush mat or a foam pad is necessary to protect your fingers from needle pricks during felting. A small amount of wool is placed on it and pierced with needles until the desired density is achieved. Experienced craftswomen advise placing a piece of viscose or other soft fabric under the wool to prevent the fibers from sinking into the brush bristles.

You will also need additional items such as templates—even cookie cutters will do—craft wire (plush, coated, or uncoated, which bends easily and retains its shape), scissors, tweezers, sewing needles and thread, beads, and other materials depending on your creativity. Additionally, thimbles and finger guards are recommended for safe working.

Safety Precautions

Please use thimbles or leather finger guards for extra protection, as the needles are very sharp.

A few rules for working with needles:
- keep the needle vertically. You should not insert the needle into the wool at one angle and pull it out at another, as this will cause it to break very quickly;
- do not use needles for wet felting, wet wool will damage them;
- do not get distracted when working with needles—this is the first rule of safety;
- to prevent injuries, it is advisable to purchase special leather or silicone thimbles for needle felting, as they will help protect your fingers from getting pricked.

Let's begin. Wishing you inspiring creativity and much enjoyment on your journey!

1. Wool Painting

Let's start with the wool! You will work with your hands and feel wool's properties. Begin by drawing with colored unspun wool.

The fibers are laid out on the base layer by layer and must be covered with glass. The resulting pictures have soft watercolor effects and are amazingly beautiful. Make use of:
- a glass frame;
- a felting surface (fabric);
- scissors, tweezers;
- wool in different colors;
- the photo of the picture.

Watch the video*

1

Place your felting surface (drap, batting, synthetic padding, or wool) on top of the cardboard frame.

*** or see page 92 for a playlist of all the videos.**

2

Lay out the wool in the background color, adjusting the height of the wool strands (or fibers) with tweezers.

3

Add dark green wool, imitating strokes. When applying it to the image, adjust it with tweezers and press it down with your hand.

4

Then lay out light green, yellow, and orange colors.

5

Cut pieces of yarn of the desired length according to the sketch and lay them out on the picture.

6

Mix strands of black, lilac, and burgundy wool on a carding brush, form small balls, and arrange the balls in the center of the dandelions as per the sketch.

7

Form circles out of white wool, adding a few lilac fibers, and arrange them around the balls.

8

Roll the tip of the white wool fibers with your fingers and add black fibers. Roll one end well and trim the top with scissors. Spread the resulting dandelion seed umbrella on the picture.

9

Cut the white wool into small pieces and arrange them around the dandelions, giving them a perfectly round shape, as shown in the sketch.

10

Use tweezers to adjust all the details of the picture and place the glass on top, tuck the wool in at the edges with tweezers and trim it with scissors if it sticks out too much.

Frame the completed work.

2. Appliqué on Clothes and Other Items

1

Wool appliqué can be done on knitted and woven woolen items, as well as on felted ones.

The fibers are laid out on the item according to the sketch and pinned with a felting needle on the front and back sides.

Try decorating a felt bag with wool. You will need:

- a brush mat, a pad;
- scissors, tweezers;
- wool;
- decor sketch;
- needles of various sizes.

2

Take a felt bag.

3

Prepare a sketch of the bag decoration on a sheet of paper. Choose a color scheme. Make the sketch in actual size, cut it out, and transfer it to the bag. Mark where the elements of the design will be located (in this example, a dolphin and waves).

4

Transfer the template outlines onto the item using a chalk or pencil, choose for yourself what to draw based on your chosen design.

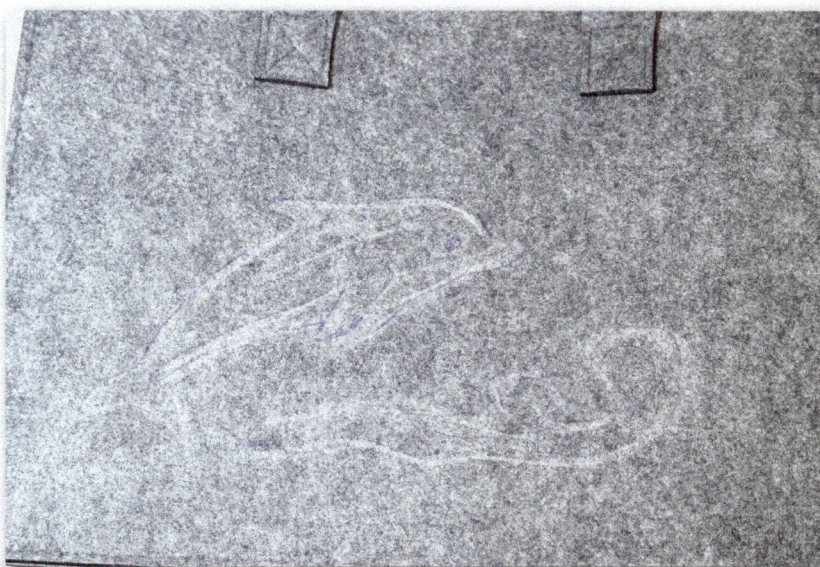

5

Take a brush mat or a foam pad (a sponge). Place it inside the bag under the pattern. First, press the fibers down from the right (front) side.

6

Based on the sketch, first lay out the lower layers of the pattern.

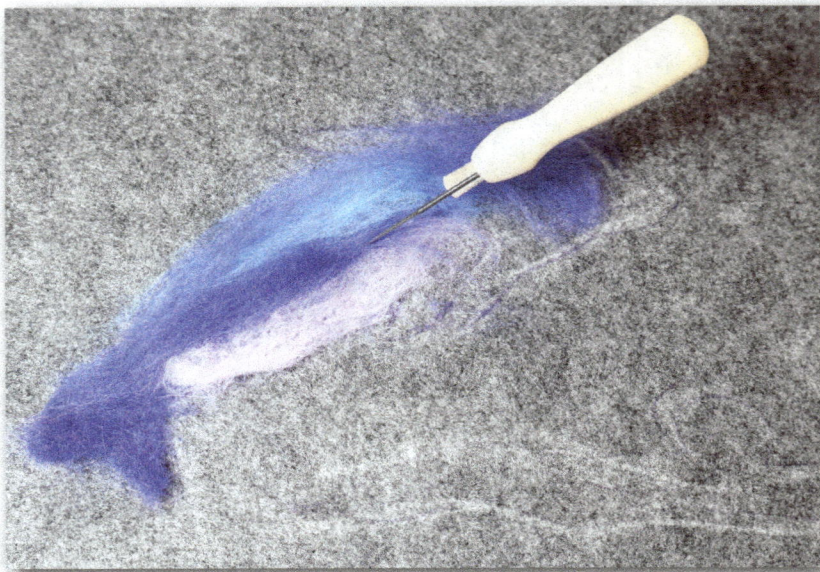

7

Turn it over to the wrong side and attach the design, if possible. Then turn it over to the right side and lay out the next layer of the design. You can roll up part of the design on the pad and then attach it to the bag.

8

Felt the waves on the pad.

9

In this way, press down the entire pattern, periodically turning it over to the wrong side to secure the fibers.

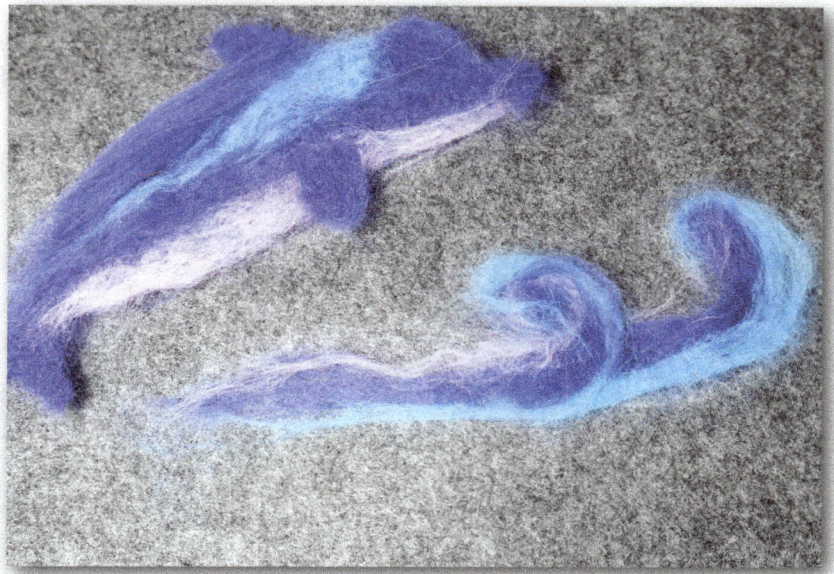

10

Use white wool fibers to create the edges of the waves and highlights on the dolphin. Use thin needles to work on small details of the design.

If the base fabric is thin and does not hold its shape well, use an embroidery hoop. The bag in this example is thick, holds its shape well, but is difficult to pierce. (You can make the appliqué separately from the base and then sew or glue it onto the item).

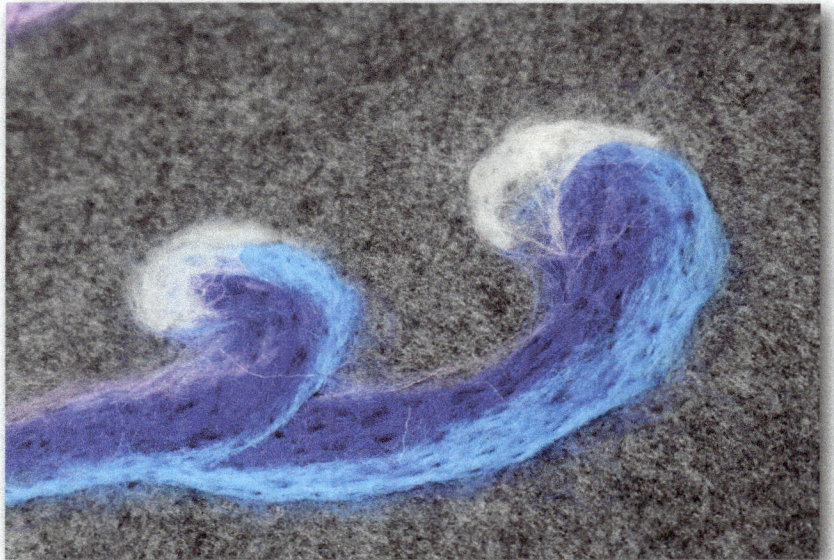

11

Done!

3. Bracelet

1

To make the bracelet, you will need:
- templates of various shapes;
- an elastic band for the bracelet;
- an awl;
- a sewing needle with a large eye;
- felting needles of various sizes;
- a pad, a brush;
- wooden beads;
- matching wool colors.

2

The bracelet will be made of woolen discs and wooden beads. Choose black beads, as they will match any wool color. The discs can be plain or melange. For melange discs, choose 2 or 3 matching wool colors. Choose either warm or cool shades.

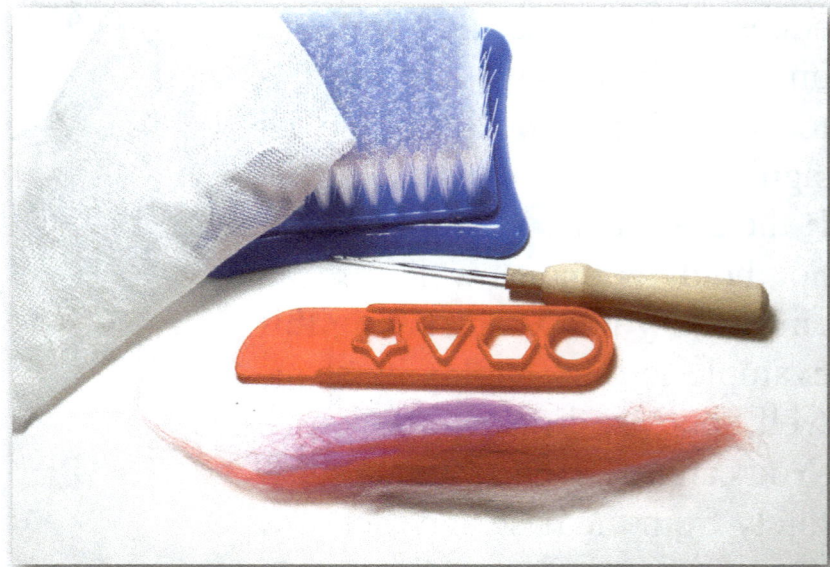

3

Take enough wool so that when you shape it into a ball, it will fit into the template. Tie the wool into a knot.

4

Place the knot in the template and pierce it with a needle, turning it over to the other side frequently. The template should be placed on a pad (a sponge) or on a brush covered with fabric.

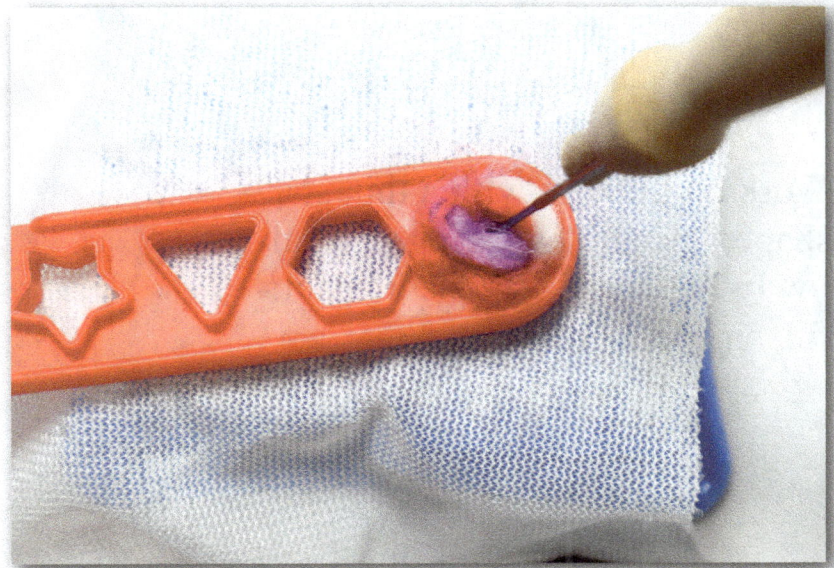

5

When the disc has been given the desired shape, treat the sides of the disc with a needle.

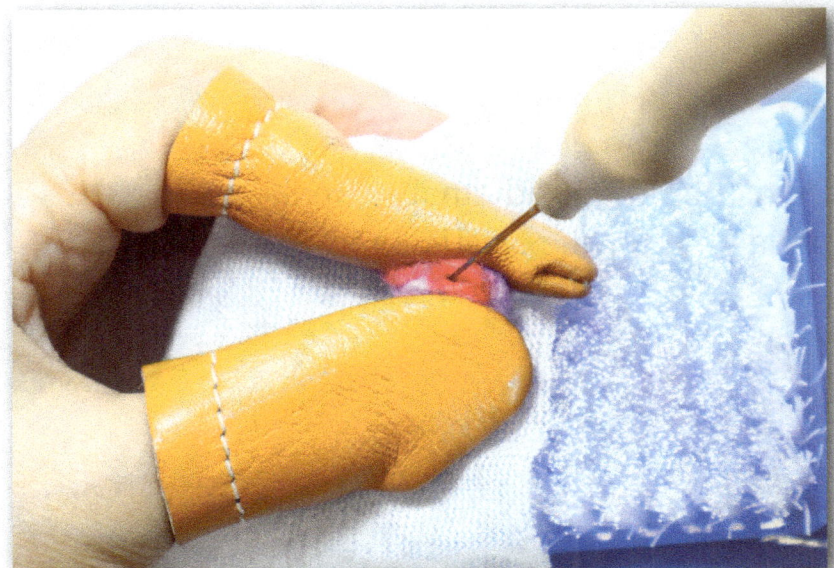

6

For added safety, hold the item between pieces of thick cardboard.

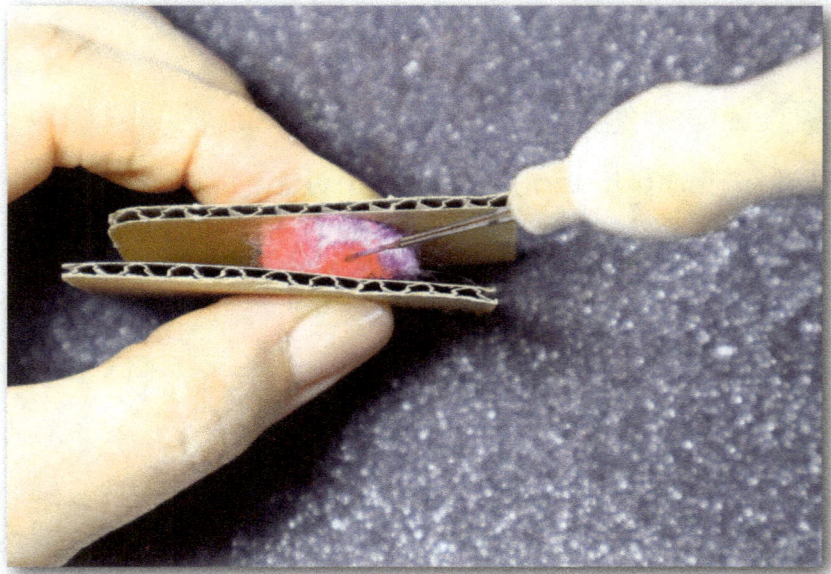

7

Work on the disc with a thin star-shaped needle, piercing it shallowly until you achieve a beautiful, smooth surface.

8

Pierce the disc with an awl, making a hole for the elastic band.

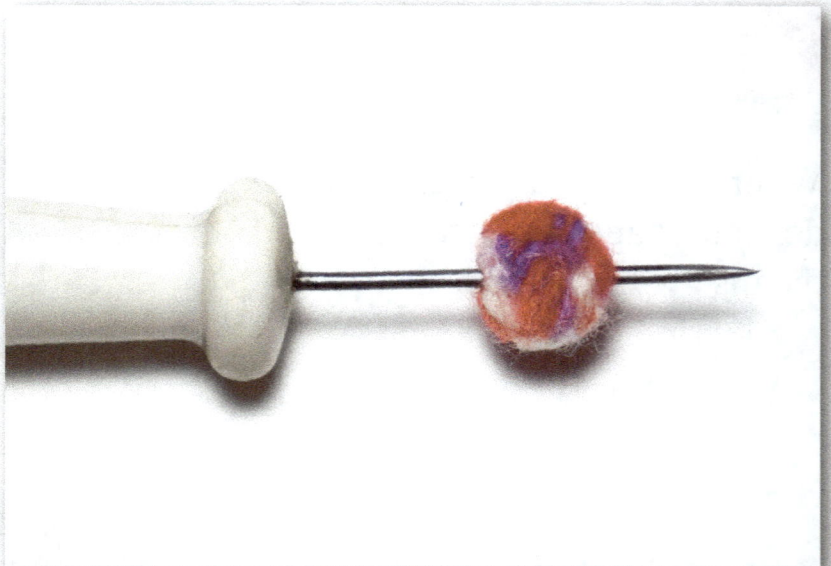

9

Thread all the bracelet parts onto the elastic band using a needle with a large eye.

10

Assemble the bracelet by alternating woolen discs and beads. You can use woolen beads of different shapes in the bracelet, such as triangles, stars, and so on, depending on your imagination and possibilities. Secure the ends of the elastic band. Instead of elastic, you can use a cord with carabiners for fastening.
Done!

4. Earrings

1

Take the wool in the color of your choice, and also prepare:
- needles of various sizes;
- fabric;
- a brush, a pad;
- thimbles;
- earring findings;
- metallic thread;
- beads;
- a long sewing needle;
- scissors;

2

Divide the wool into two equal pieces.

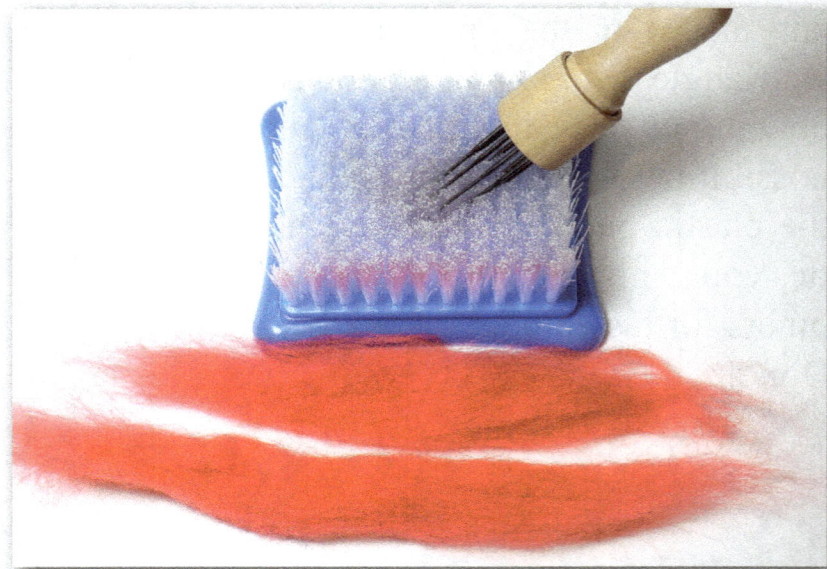

3

Roll the wool into a knot.

4

Wrap the tail of the knot around a ball of wool, place it on the brush, and then begin to pierce it repeatedly with the needle handle, turning it over constantly.

5

Cover the brush with fabric to prevent the fibers from falling into it. Then pierce it with a thick triangular needle, paying attention to the protruding parts and adding wool in small strands. Make the punctures shallow and as close to each other as possible. The more punctures there are, the smoother the surface will be.

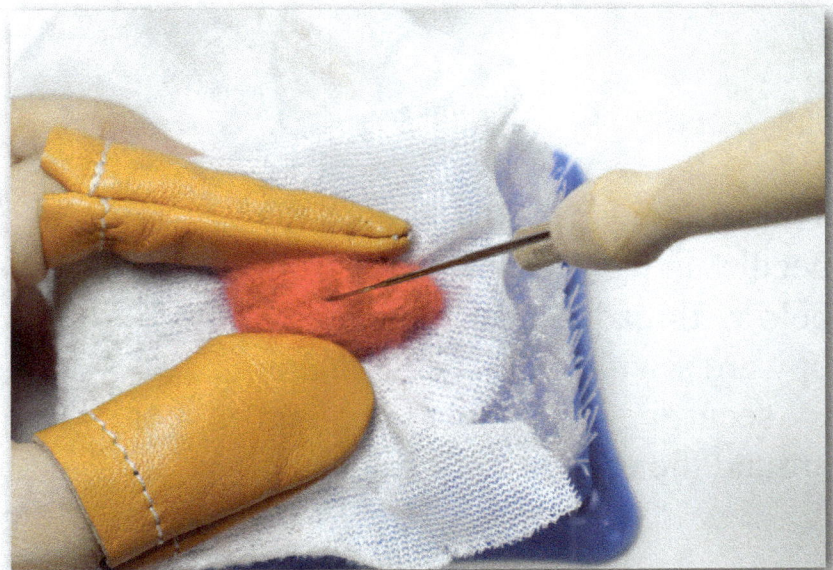

6

Continue until you have a tear-drop shape that is smooth on all sides. If it does not deform when pressed, then you have done everything correctly.

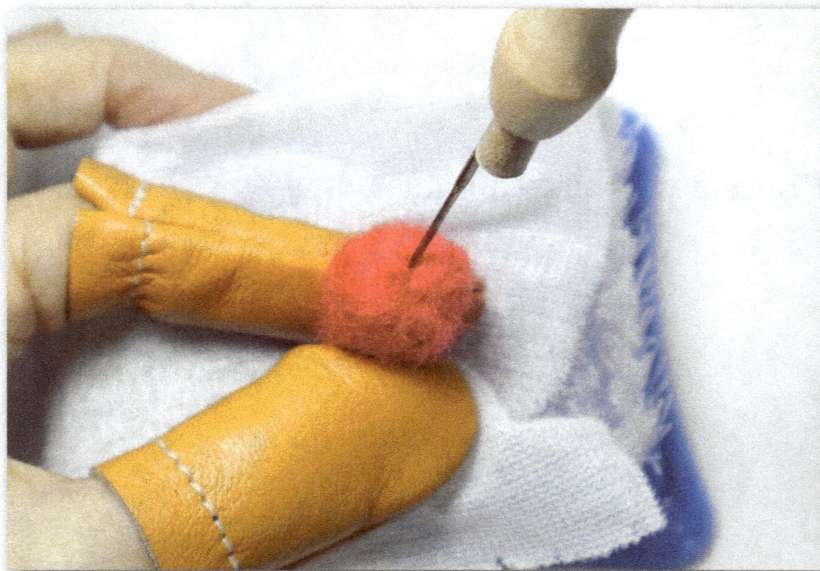

7

To make a teardrop for an earring, take some lurex, metallic thread, earring findings, and a long sewing needle. Thread the needle and pierce the teardrop exactly in the middle from bottom to top.

8

Thread the earring parts onto the needle and go back down. From below, thread a bead and pierce upwards with the needle again to secure everything. Then, go around the earring with stitches.

9

Make another earring.

10

Decorate the item as you wish. You can also make a pendant in the same way.

5. Needle Felting a Lily Flower

1

To make a flower, you will need:
- a brush, a pad;
- fabric;
- needles of various thicknesses;
- thimbles and thick cardboard;
- white, pink, and lilac wool.

2

Disentangle the white wool and place it on the brush, then pierce it with a thick triangular needle, shaping it into a petal. Hold the needle at a right angle to ensure that the punctures are even and deep. Turn the petal over to the other side several times. Use a multi-needle holder to work faster.

3

Disentangle a few strands of lilac and pink wool.

4

Place the fibers on the base of the petal. Pin them down with needles on both sides.

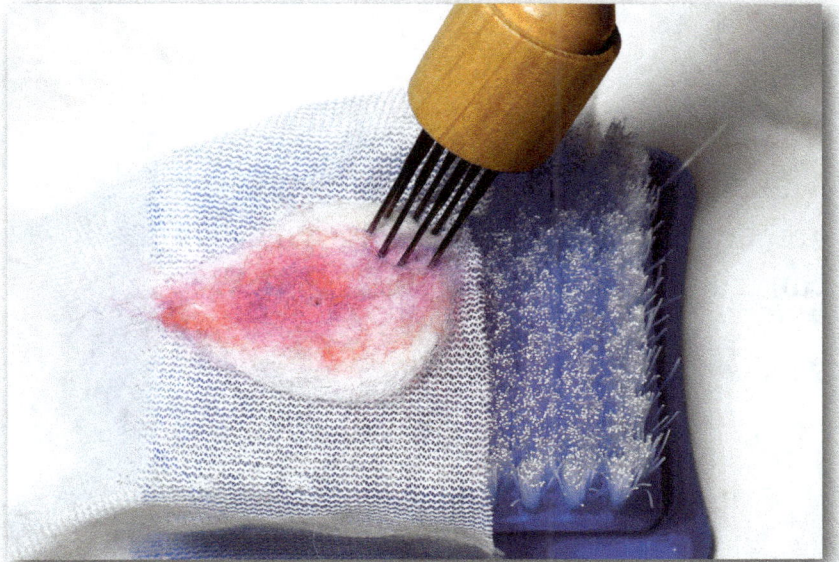

5

Craft the petals with a thin star needle on a backing, then polish them.

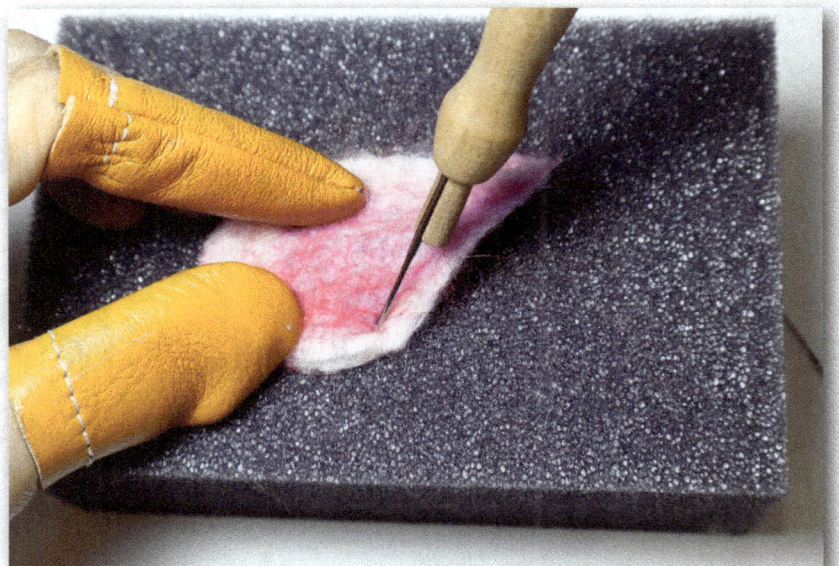

6

Work the petals from the ends with a needle, holding them between pieces of cardboard.

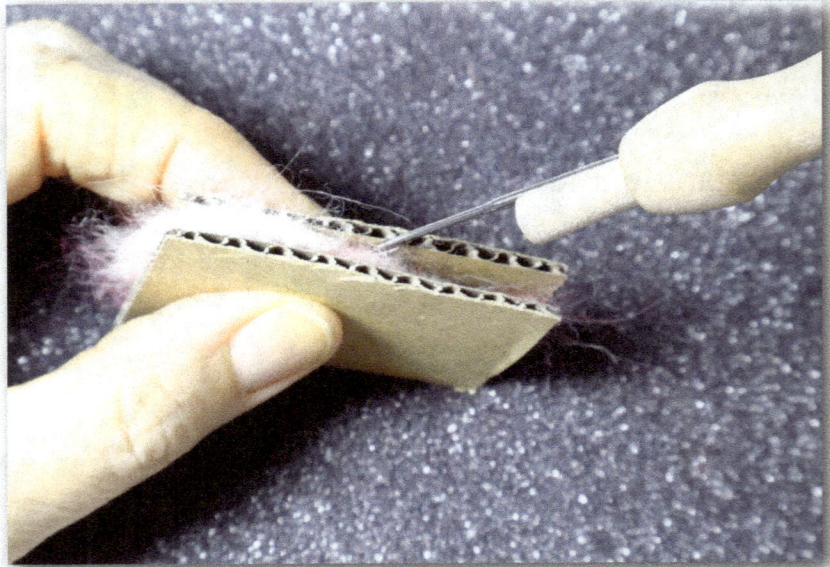

7

Make 8 petals this way. If there are any fibers sticking out, you can trim them with scissors.

8

For the stamens, roll a small amount of white wool in your palms. Pierce them with a thin needle, make 2 balls of green wool and attach them to the white wool on both sides.

9

Make another stamen.

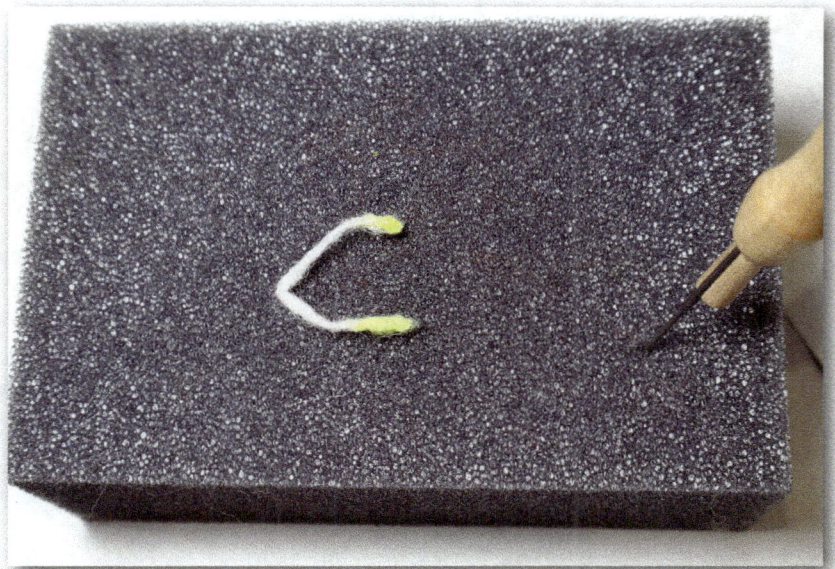

10

Make the center of the flower from yellow wool using a template (see bracelet).

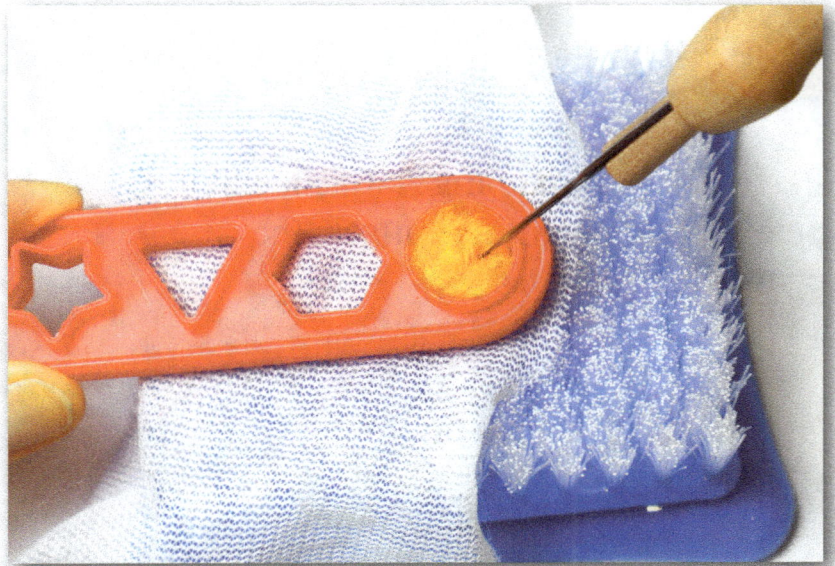

11

Connect 4 petals by piercing them with a needle along the edge, folding them inside out.

12

Connect the center and petals by piercing them with a needle.

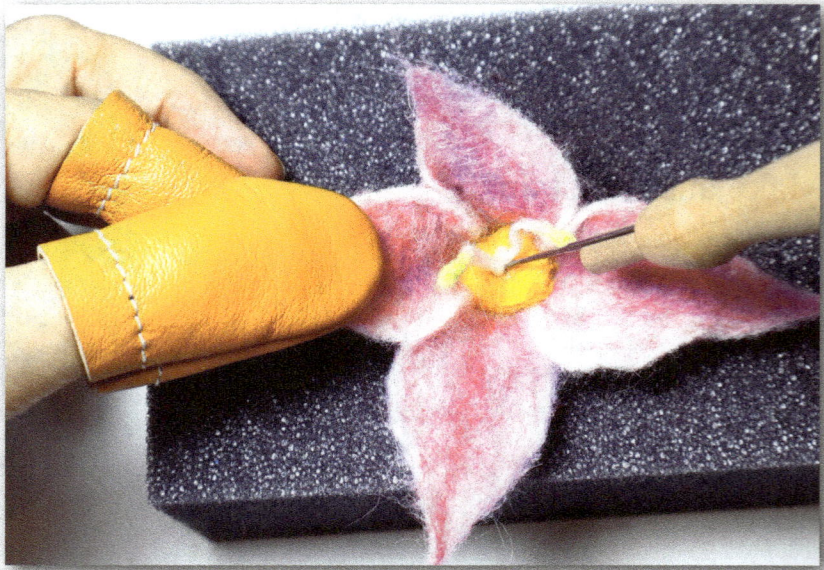

13

Place the remaining attached petals underneath and attach the center and stamens.

14

Turn the flower over and pierce the center of the flower with a thin needle, folding the petals together.

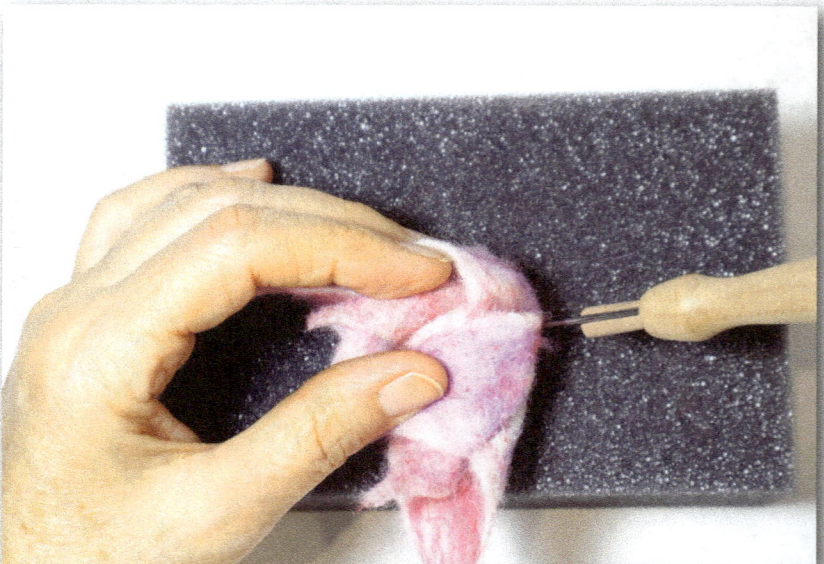

You can sew a pin to this flower and wear it as a brooch.

6. Felting a Wire-Based Flower

1

You will need:
- 0.4 mm (about 0.015 in) thick craft wire;
- needles of various thicknesses;
- a brush, a pad;
- scissors;
- orange, white, yellow, dark green, and light green wool.

2

Cut 5–6 pieces of wire, 20–25 cm (around 7.87–9.84 in) long. Roll them into rings and twist the ends together.

3

Disentangle the wool and place it on the brush (covered with fabric), then pierce it with a thick triangular needle or a multi-needle holder. Hold it at a right angle so that the punctures are even and deep. Turn the plate over to the other side several times.

4

Place the wire on the wool and, bending the edges around the wire, pierce it again with a multi-needle holder until you get a petal.

5

Place a little white and yellow wool on the base of the petal and secure it with needles on both sides.

6

Make 5–6 petals this way.

7

For the stamens, cut 25–30 cm (9.84–11.8 in) of wire, pierce a strip of yellow wool, and wrap it around the middle of the wire. Pierce carefully with a needle.

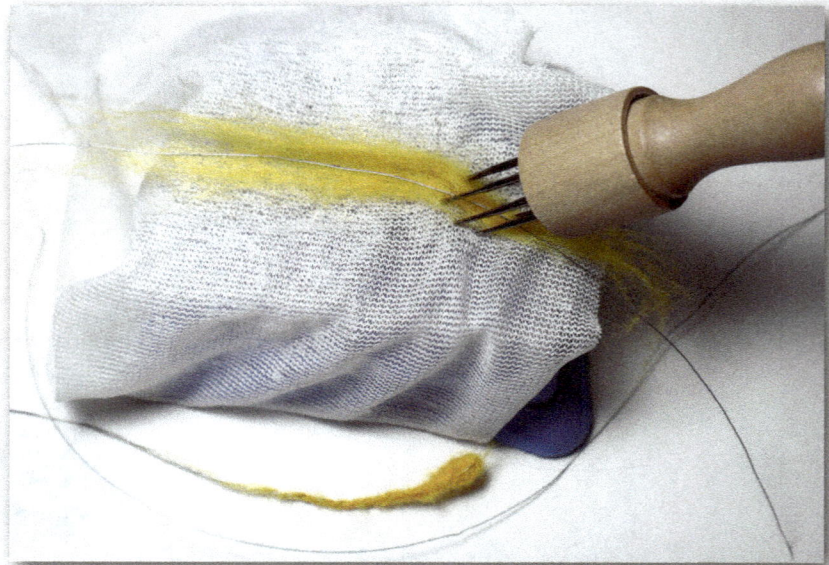

8

Fold the item in half and twist it. Make 3 such pieces.

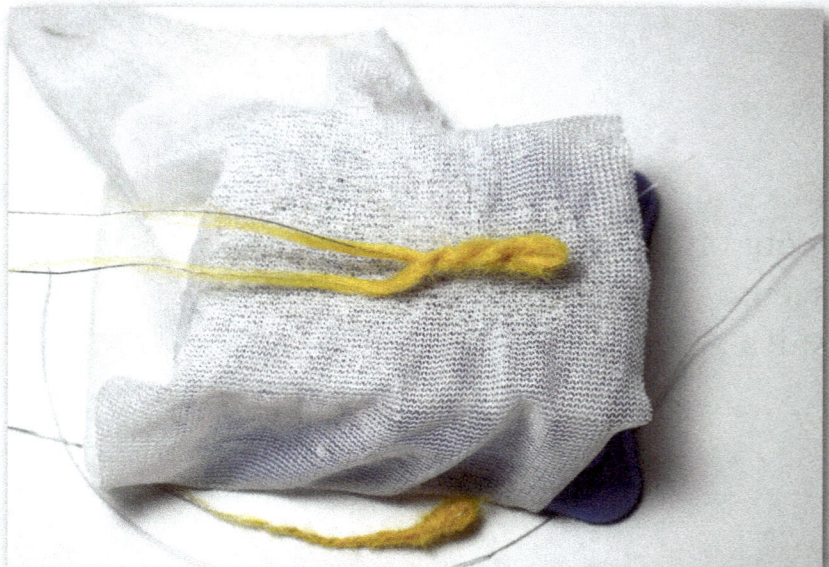

9

Place the stamens on the petal, twisting at the base.

10

Add the remaining petals, forming a flower. Twist the ends into a stem.

11

Disentangle the light and dark green wool and place it on the brush, then pierce the strip of wool with a needle.

12

Wrap a strip of wool around the stem of the flower and pierce it, securing the wool around the wire.

13

Shape the flower into a beautiful form. You can also add leaves.

7. Owl the Brooch

1

To make this brooch, you will need:
- needles of various thicknesses;
- a brush;
- a pad;
- scissors;
- beige, burgundy, white and yellow wool;
- eyes and a brooch pin.

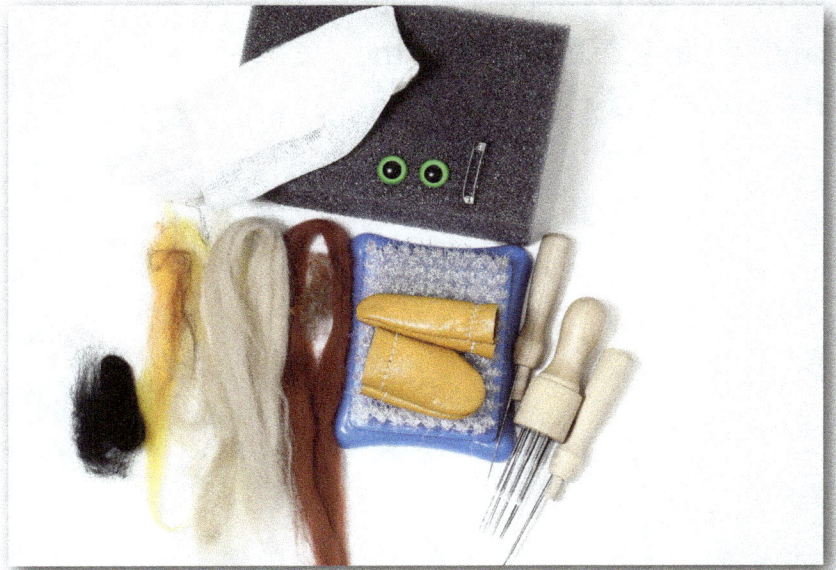

2

Roll the beige wool into an oval shape. Pierce it thoroughly with a needle holder on both sides until it becomes dense.

3

With a thin needle, shape the owl's neck, separating the head from the body.

4

Apply glue to the eyes and stick them onto the head.

5

Attach burgundy wool fibers to the neck and white fibers above the eyes to make eyebrows.

6

Attach light wool fibers around the eyes for feathers.

7

Attach the burgundy wool above the eyebrows and trim it. Attach the black wool for the beak.

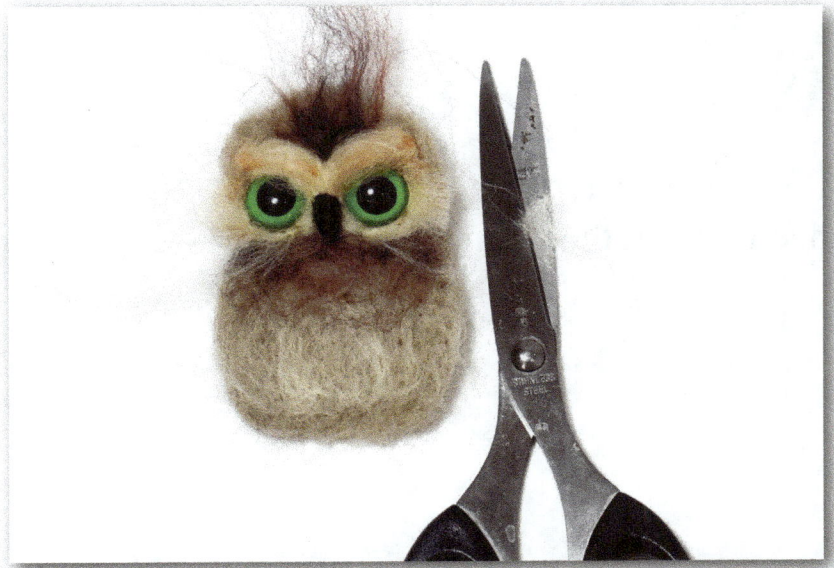

8

On the back side, attach black wool along the edge of the head.

9

Attach light-colored wool to the bottom of the item from the front side and add burgundy dots on the owl's belly.

10

Pin the burgundy dots with a thin needle from the wrong side.

11

Make dark feathers on the head.

12

Pierce through with a thin needle from the other side, securing the pattern.
Sew the pin on.

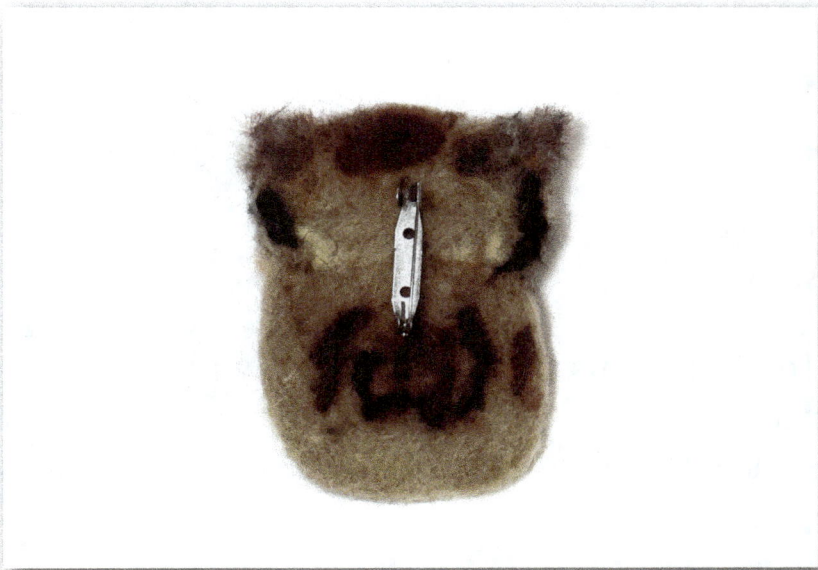

13

The brooch is done!

8. Hedgehog the Needle Holder

1

To make this hedgehog, you will need:
- needles of various thicknesses,
- a brush;
- a pad;
- a piece of fabric;
- wool in the color of your choice, light for the base and dark for the back;
- finger guards.

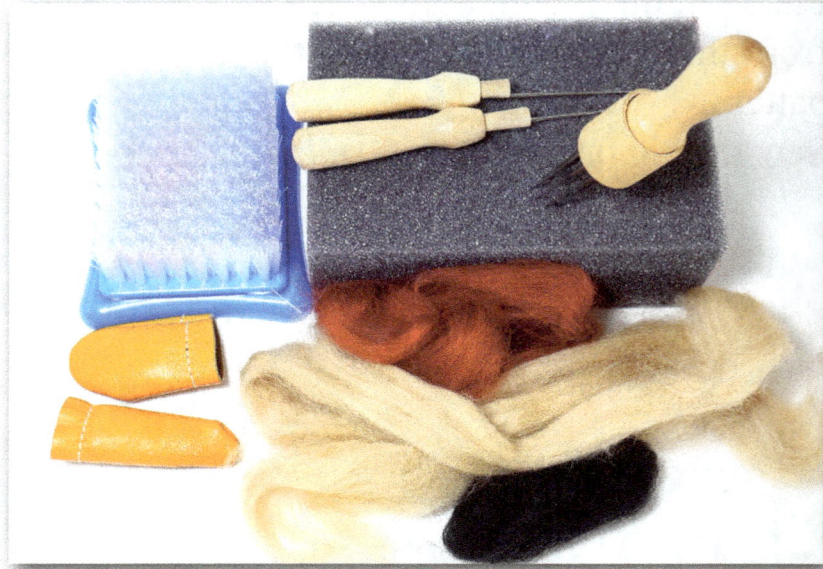

2

Take a bunch of wool, keeping in mind that it will shrink significantly during felting. Squeeze the wool in your fist to determine the size of the future item. Roll the wool into a tight, large knot. Spread the ends over the knot.

3

Shape the lump into an oval, place it on a brush, and pierce it repeatedly with the needle holder. Put on the finger guards.

4

Turn the ball of wool and pierce it until it forms an ellipsoid shape. Shape the ball of wool to form the body of the hedgehog, as in sculpting. Add wool as needed.

5

Disentangle the black and burgundy wool on a carding brush, mixing the fibers together. You can use brown wool if you'd like.

6

Place the wool on the brush and pierce it thoroughly with a multi-needle holder. If the fibers fall into the brush, cover it with fabric or use a foam pad.

7

Place the resulting layer on the hedgehog and pierce it with a thin needle, connecting the wool to the body.

8

Take two small pieces of light-colored wool for the ears, pierce holes in the layers, tucking the wool with a needle from the edge to the center to form the ears. Leave loose fibers on one side of each ear.

9

Attach the ears to the hedgehog's body with a thin needle. At the point where the ears are attached, tuck any loose fibers into the hedgehog's body with the needle. Place a small, thin strand of dark wool on top of the back of the ears so that it covers both pieces (the ears and the body), and carefully attach it with the needle.

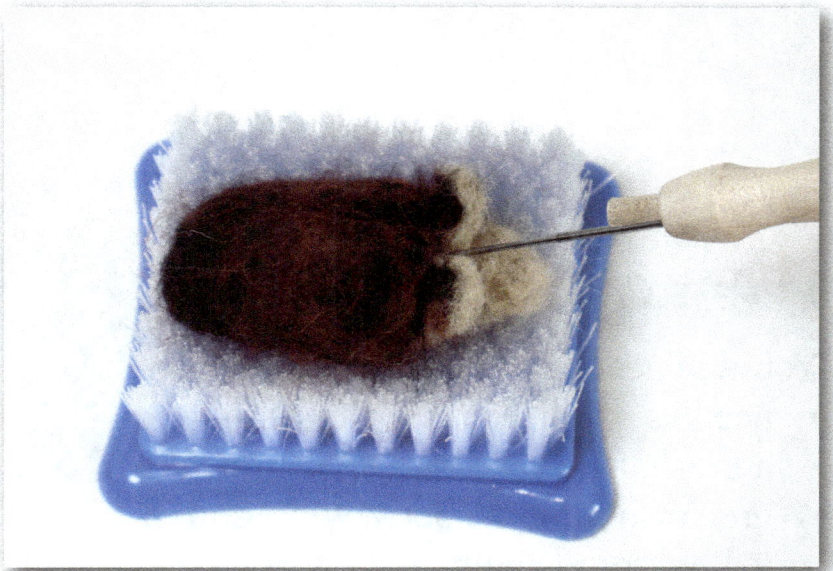

10

Attach several strands of light-colored wool in the eye areas, then attach strands of black wool to one spot for the eyes. Carefully stitch black wool at the very tip for the nose. Pierce with a needle at only one spot.
Make the eyes sparkle by sticking pins into them.

11

The needle holder is done!

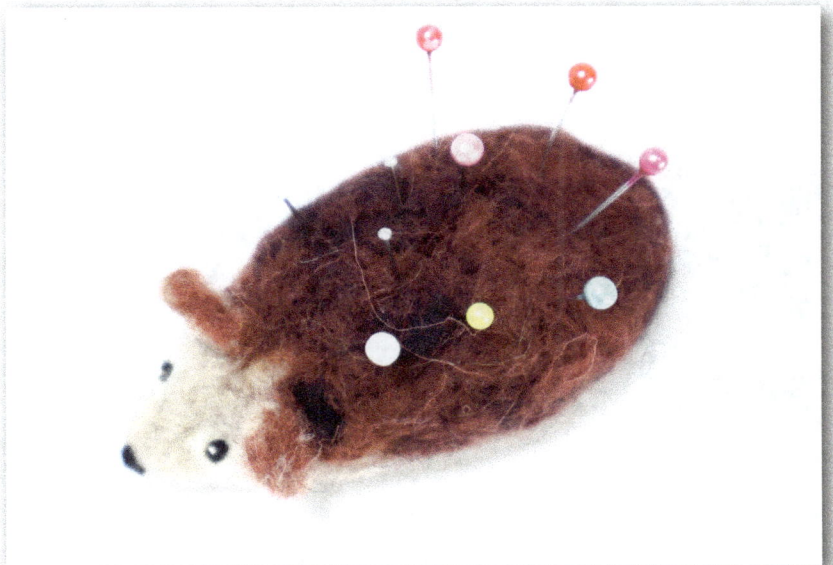

9. Frog

1

You will need:
- needles of various thicknesses;
- a brush, a pad;
- green wool for the body, white and yellow for the belly and eyes;
- beads for the eyes;
- a sewing needle and thread.

2

Roll the wool into a lump and spread the ends over it.

3

Shape the lump into a ball, place it on the brush, and pierce it repeatedly with a needle holder, turning the lump of wool. Pierce until you get a dense ball, shaped like a frog's body.

4

Now take a medium-sized needle and start adding wool in small strands. Make the punctures shallow and as close to each other as possible. The more punctures you make, the smoother the surface will be. Use frequent, thin, shallow punctures to tangle the fibers, creating a smooth, dense surface.

5

Take 4 balls of wool for the legs. Each part of the item requires its own piece of wool. Then attach the pieces to each other.

6

Leave a few loose fibers at the joint on one of the pieces. Thread them through the other piece with a needle.

7

Place a small thin strand on top so that it covers both pieces, and carefully attach it with a needle. Attach all the legs to the frog's body.

8

Take the yellow wool and make a round piece for the belly, place it on the brush, poking it repeatedly with a needle holder.

9

Attach the belly.

10

Felt green circles for the eyes and slightly smaller white ones.

11

Connect the pieces for the eyes and sew beads onto them.

12

Finally, attach the eyes to the frog's body in the same way as you attached the other parts.

13

Use a thin needle to attach a few strands of black wool for the mouth.

14

The frog is done.

10. Snowman the Christmas Tree Ornament

1

You will need:
- needles of various thicknesses;
- a brush;
- a pad;
- white wool, yellow and red for the hat, black for the eyes, orange for the nose, and purple for the scarf;
- beads and an ornament hook;
- a long sewing needle and thread.

2

Take white wool, gather it into an oblong ball, place it on the brush, and pierce it repeatedly with a needle holder.

3

On the pad, use a triangular needle to create a dense roll. Then pierce it with a thick triangular needle. Pay attention to the protruding parts, adding wool in small strands. Make the punctures shallow, as close to each other as possible. The more punctures, the smoother the surface will be.

4

Pierce the neck with a thin needle. Craft and sand the entire surface of the toy with a thin star-shaped needle.

5

Use the red wool on the brush, and with a needle holder, shape a flat piece for the hat.

6

Felt a yellow strip for the hat trim.

7

Felt an orange carrot for the nose.

8

Attach the hat to the snowman and carefully attach the nose with a thin needle. Attach a few strands of black wool (for the eyes and mouth).

9

Felt the strip for the scarf.

10

Wrap the scarf around the snowman's neck and secure it to the body by piercing it with a thin needle. Trim the ends of the scarf with scissors.

11

Take a sewing needle with white thread and sew on the beads like buttons.

52

Sew on the ornament hook, and the toy is done.

11. Snail

1

Take wool in different colors of your choice. For the snail in this example, burgundy, orange, yellow, beige, a little red, and green wool is used. You will also need:

- a pad;
- needles;
- a brush;
- thimbles;
- fabric;
- a small piece of foam rubber.

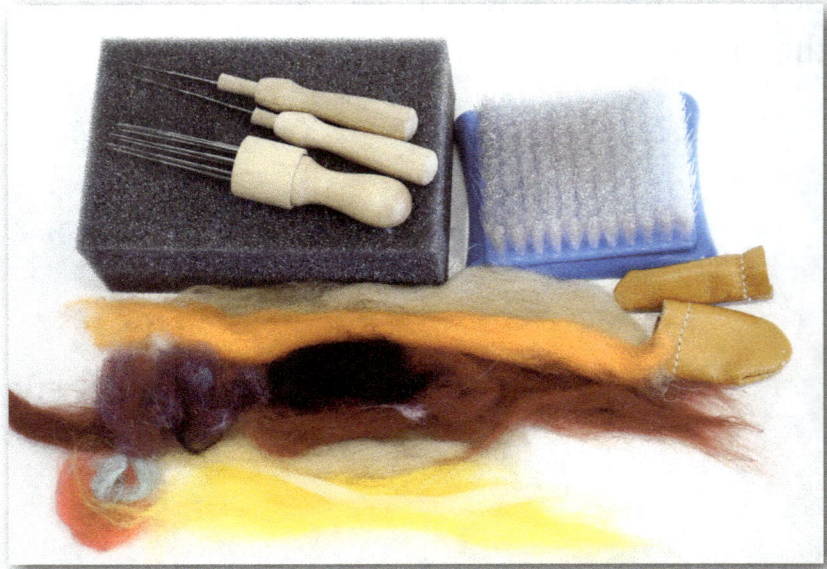

2

Fold the wool of all colors into a strip.Place the strip on the brush and pierce it with a needle handle. Make the strip dense and thick.

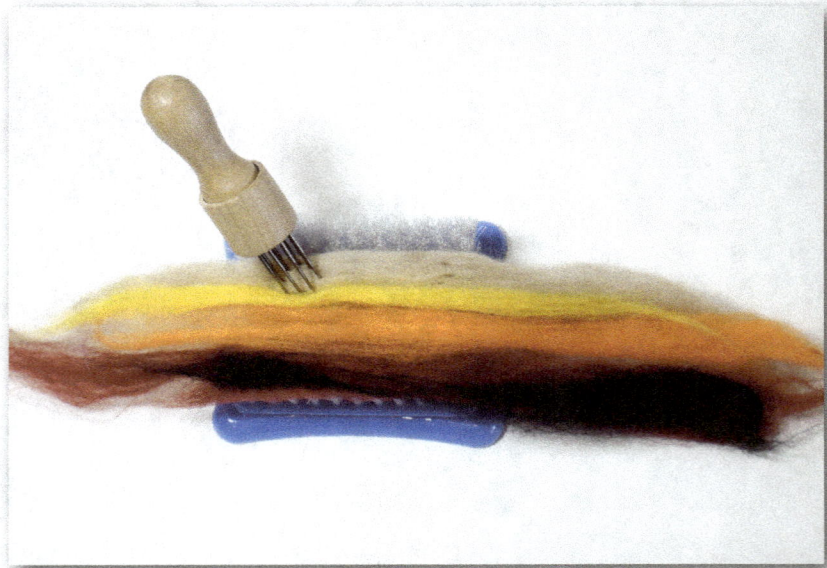

3

Roll the strip into a spiral ring and fasten it with a thin needle. Make the edges of the shell.

4

Take a sponge or foam rubber and roll it into a roll.

5

Place the foam rubber inside the shell and secure the edges of the shell by piercing them with a needle.

6

Make the bottom of the shell by piercing a piece of wool on the brush, turning it over several times.

7

Attach the bottom of the shell to the edges on the outside and inside.

8

Turn the piece inside out and pierce it with a needle, forming a shell, several times, achieving a good, strong shape.

9

For the snail's body, mix yellow, orange, and beige wool.

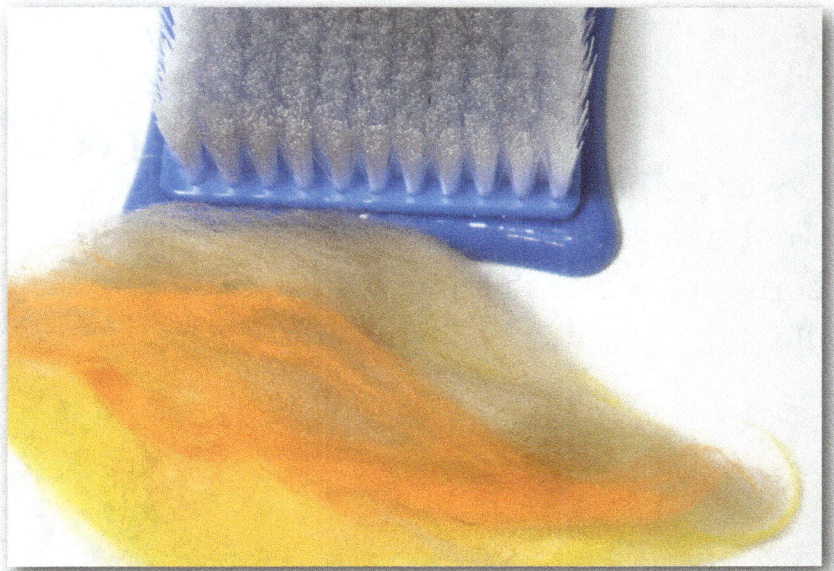

10

Place the wool on the brush and shape a cord using a multi-needle holder.

11

Make a knot at one end and form the snail's head with a needle.

12

Cover the head with light-colored wool and sew it on. Pull out the horns and pierce them with a needle.

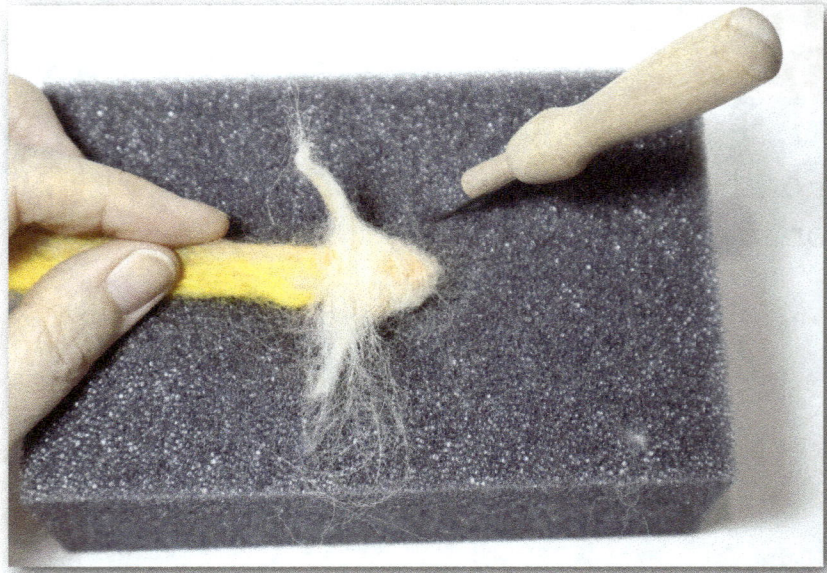

13

Make two small green balls for the eyes and attach them onto the horns. To prevent the wool from falling into the brush, cover it with fabric.

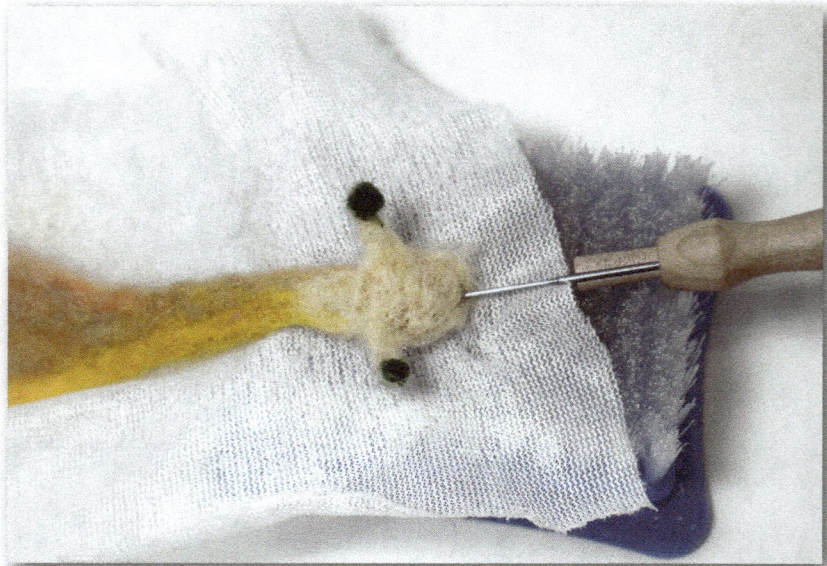

14

Attach the shell to the snail's body.

15

Turn it inside out and attach everything securely again.

16

Attach the snail's neck to the shell, then turn it right side out. Make a stable shape.

17

Use a thin needle to make a mouth out of several strands of red wool.

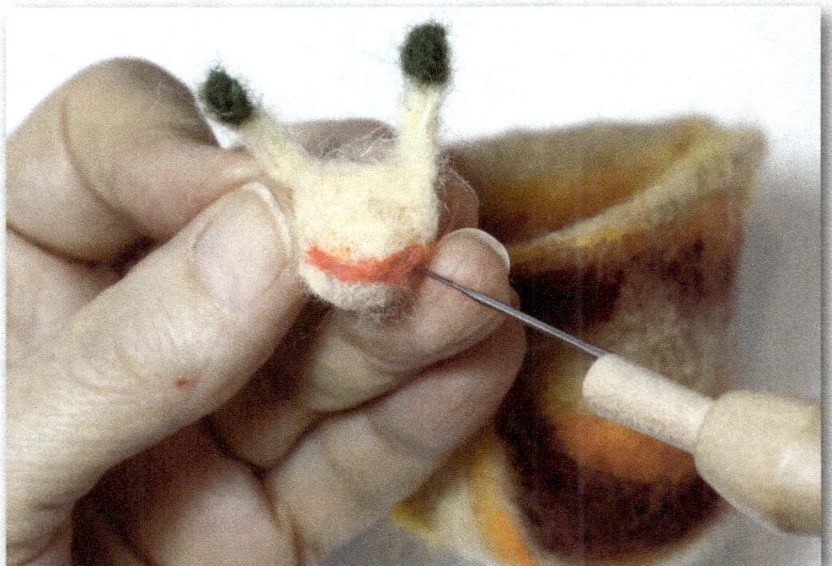

The snail is done! It can be used as a box for jewelry or other small items.

12. Rabbit

1

To make this toy, take gray wool, white and pink wool for the belly and nose, and brown wool for the paws and ears. You will also need:

- a pad;
- needles;
- a brush, fabric;
- thimbles;
- a sewing needle;
- thread;
- beads for the eyes.

2

Body. Take a strand of wool, clench it in your fist, and feel the volume of the future toy. Make one knot in the middle of the strand and another small knot at the end of the strand. Spread the ends of the knots.

3

Hide the knots in the wool to give the lump a pear shape.

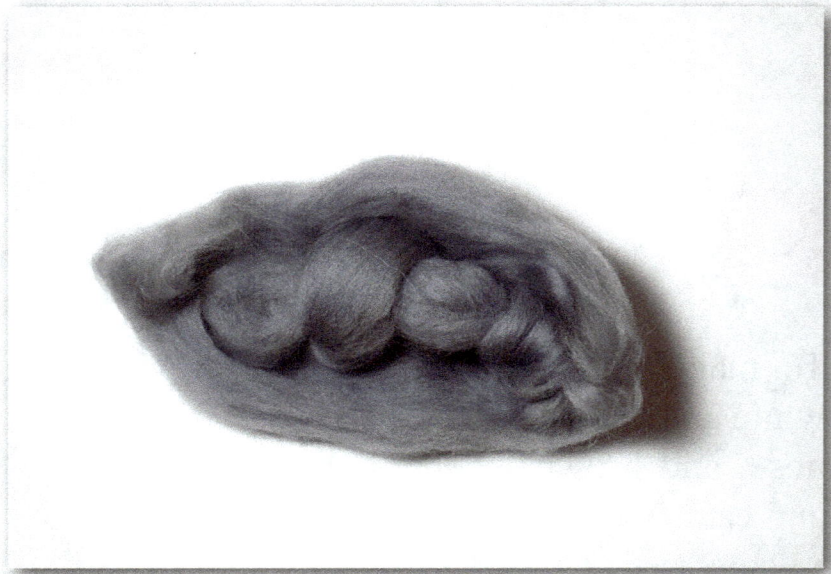

4

Place the piece on the brush and pierce it with the needle holder.

5

Turn the ball of wool around and pierce it until you get a dense pear-shaped piece.

6

Belly. Take white wool, place it on the brush, and make an oval piece for the belly by piercing it with a multi-needle holder. Attach the belly to the bunny's body.

7

Take two strands of wool for the ears. Felt the ears, leaving loose strands at one end to attach them to the head.

8

Attach the ears to the head with a thin needle and an extra strand of gray wool.

9

Attach a piece of dark or white wool to the ears.

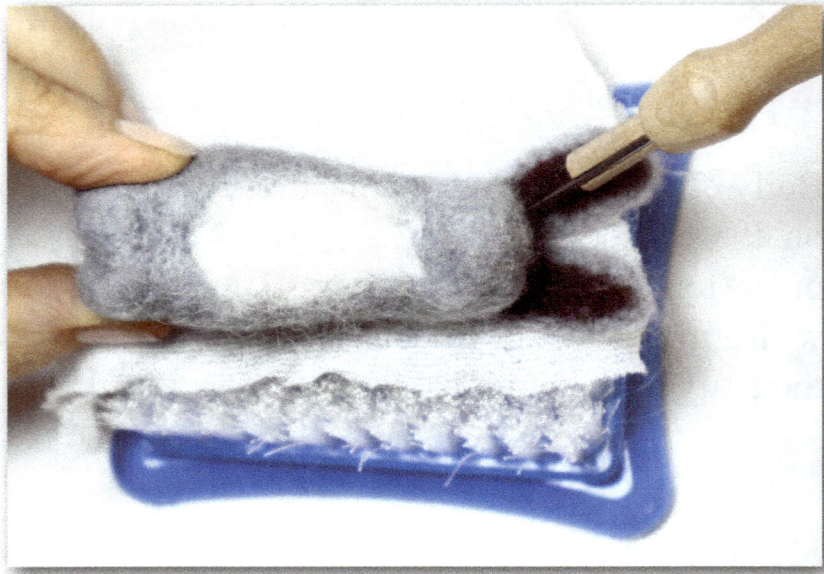

10

Muzzle. Shape the head, actively piercing the neck area.

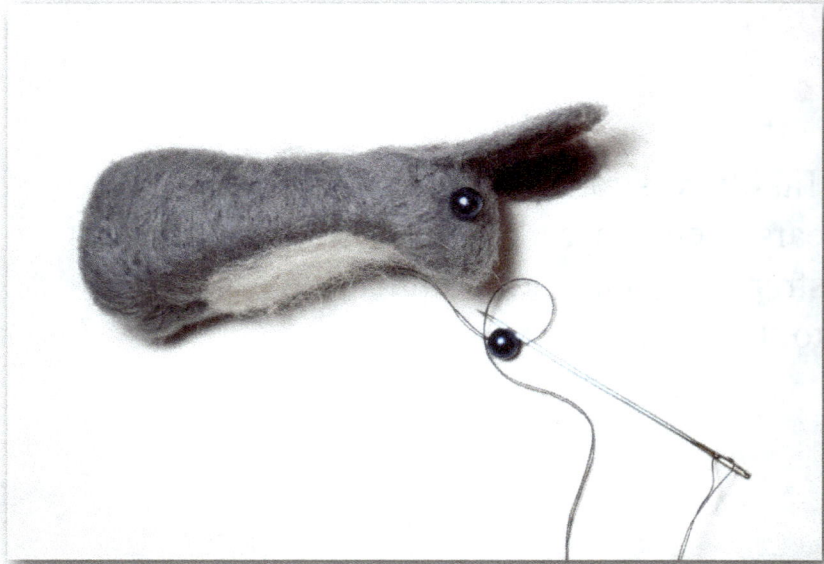

11

Sew the bead eyes to the head with a sewing needle, pulling them tightly together.

12

Attach a strand of wool as eyebrows above the eyes.

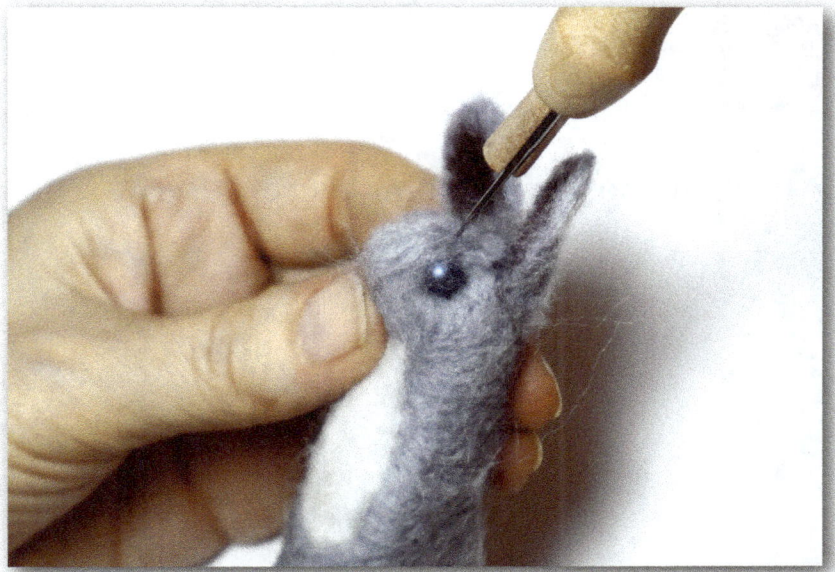

13

Attach a thin strip of white wool around the eyes.

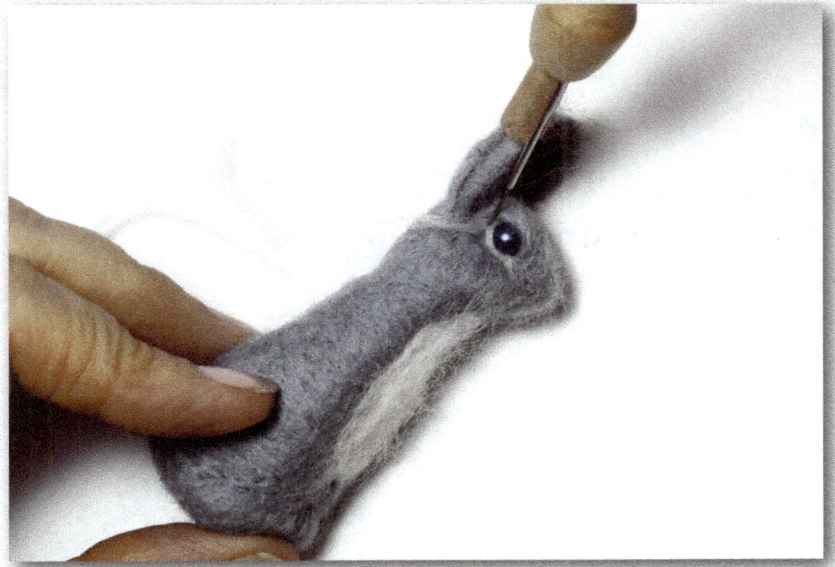

14

Felt four small white balls for the face (two cheeks, chin, and nose) and a red one for the nose.

15

Attach the nose with a pink piece.

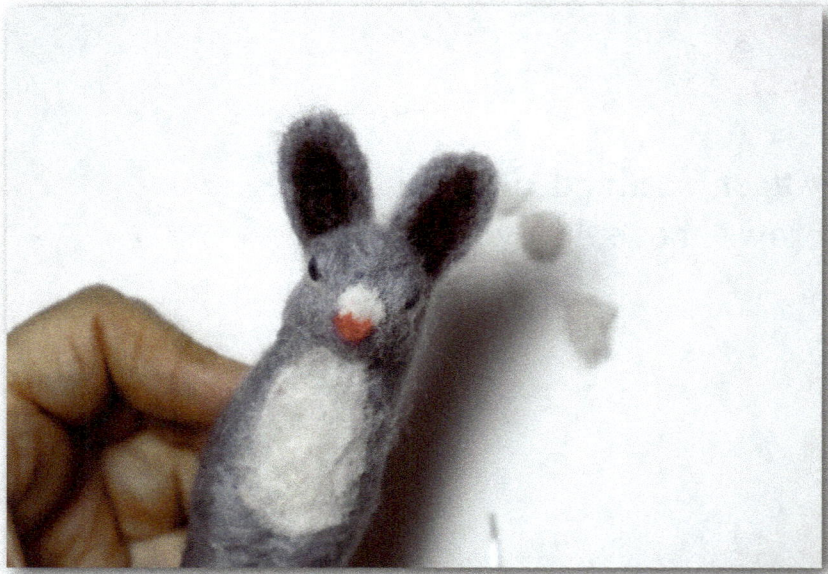

16

Then attach the cheeks and chin. Attach a red strip for the mouth.

17

Felt two pairs of legs. Make the hind legs shorter. Leave loose fibers at their ends to connect them to the body.

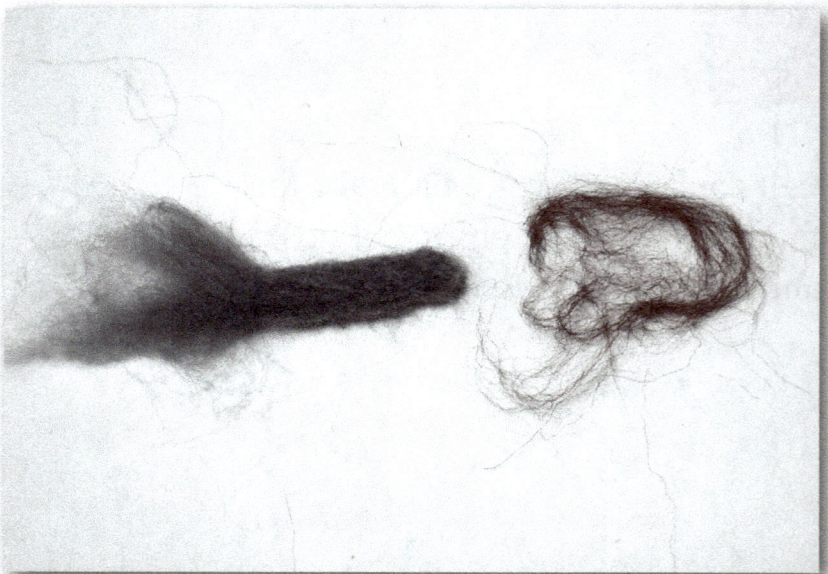

18

Stuff the ends of the paws with dark or white wool.

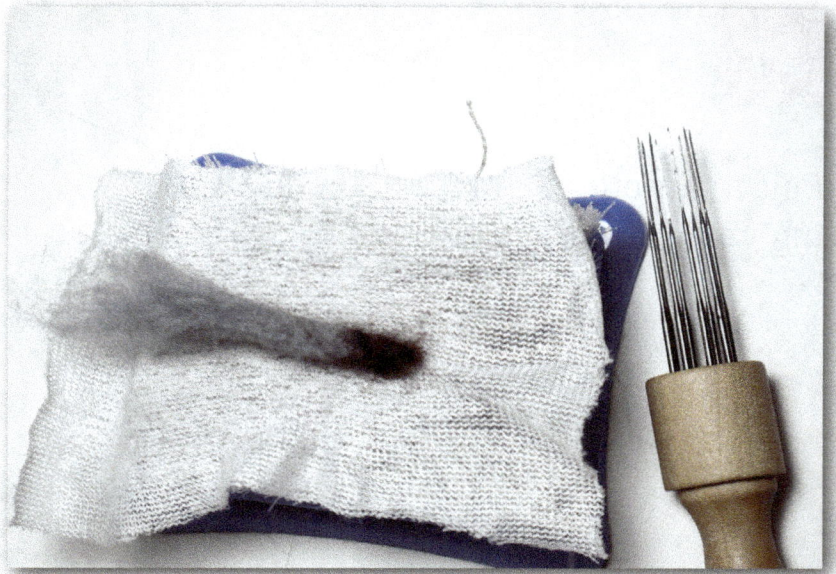

19

Attach the legs to the body.

20

Add more wool to the back, smoothing the surface.

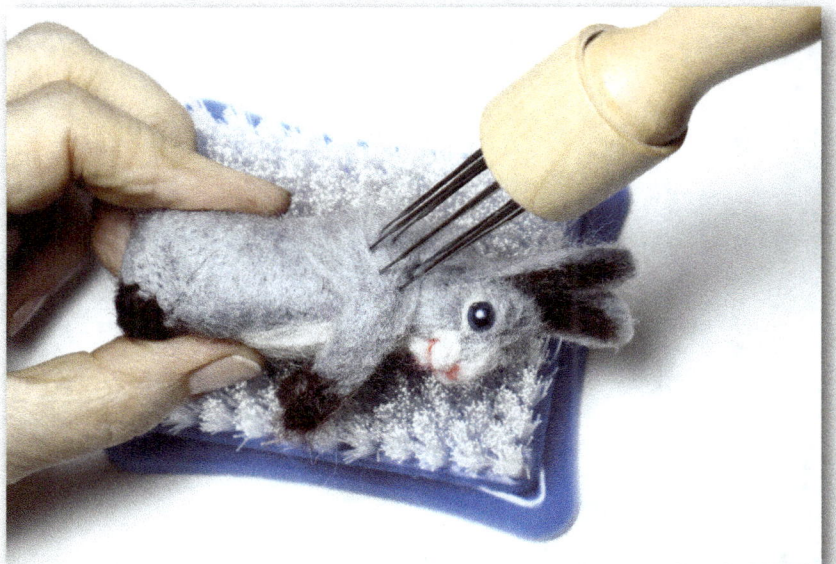

21

Felt a tail out of gray wool, adding white wool.

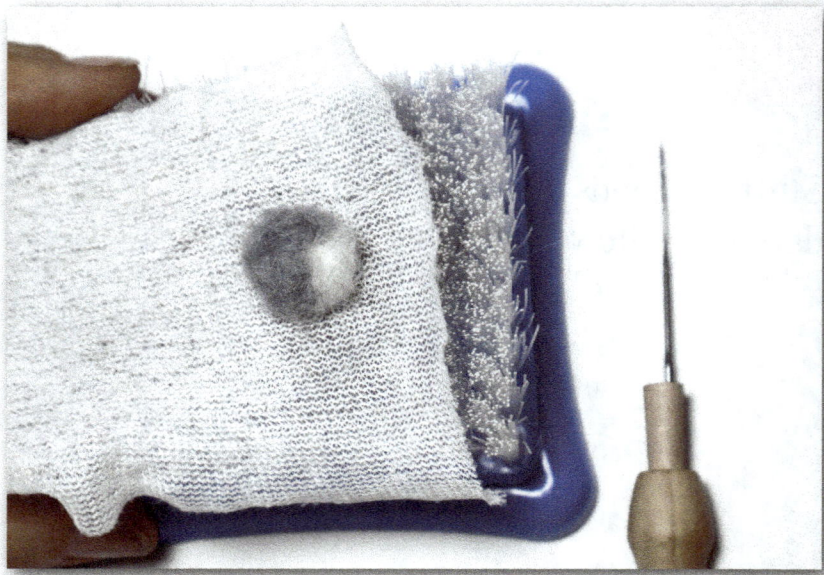

22

Attach the tail to the bunny's body using gray wool fibers.

Finish the item with a thin needle.

The bunny is done.

13. Dog

1

You will need:
- needles of various thicknesses;
- a brush, a pad;
- beige and brown wool for the eyes, black for the nose;
- 0.4 mm (about 0.015 in) craft wire;
- scissors;
- toothpicks.

2

Cut three pieces of wire, each 30 cm (about 11.8 in) long.

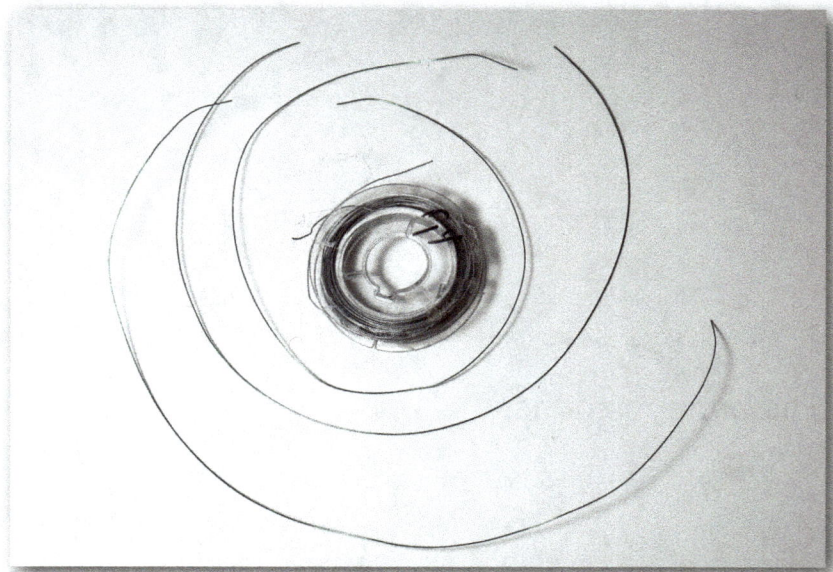

3

Connect each piece into a ring, then squeeze in the middle and twist to form a stick with loops at the ends.

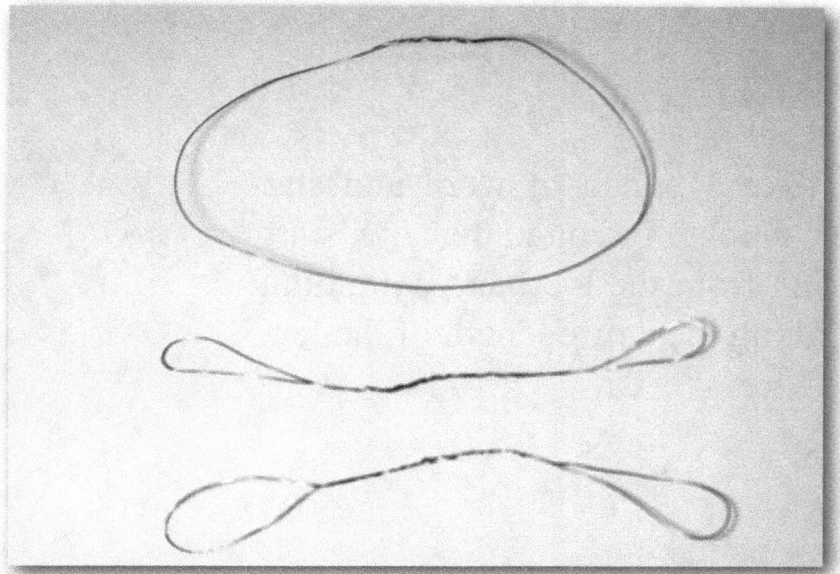

4

Connect these three pieces by twisting two around one. Use pliers to make the connection stronger. Clamp the twisted area.

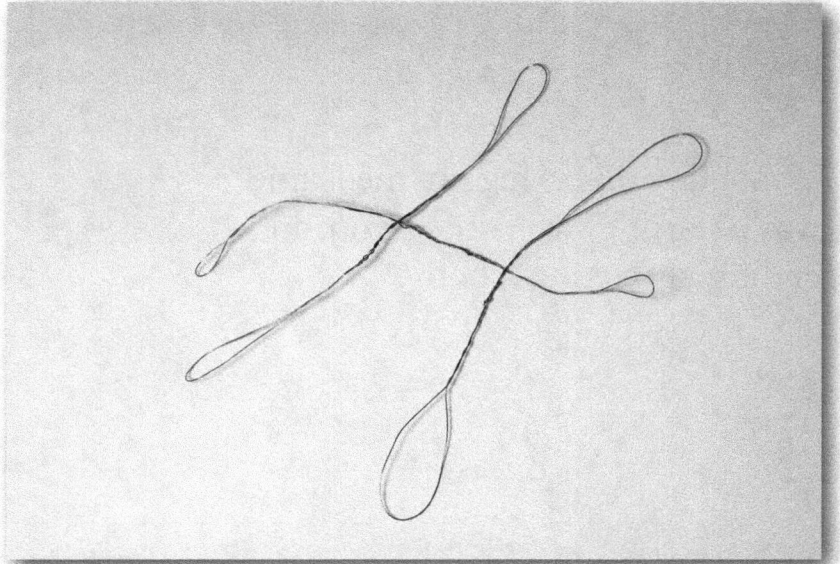

5

Bend the ends to form the dog's skeleton.

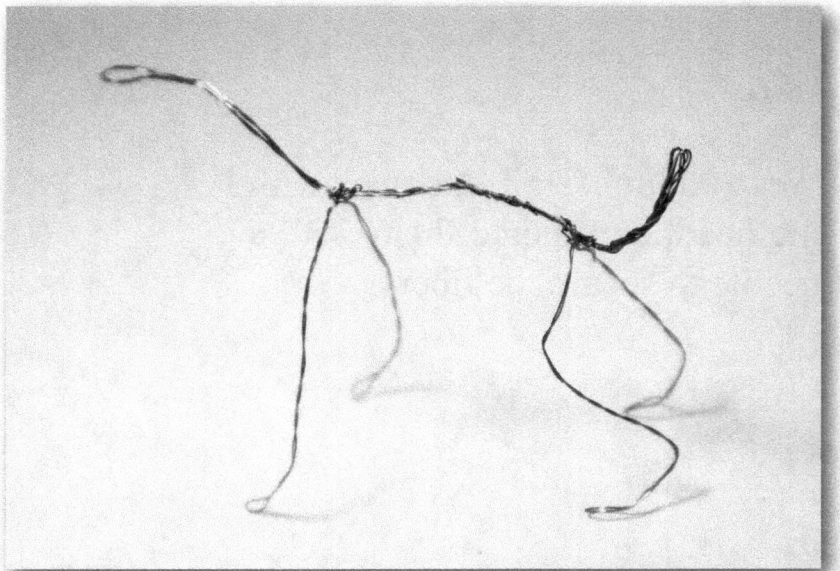

6

Take a bunch of wool and start wrapping it around the wire, starting from the loop and continuing along the entire length of the leg.

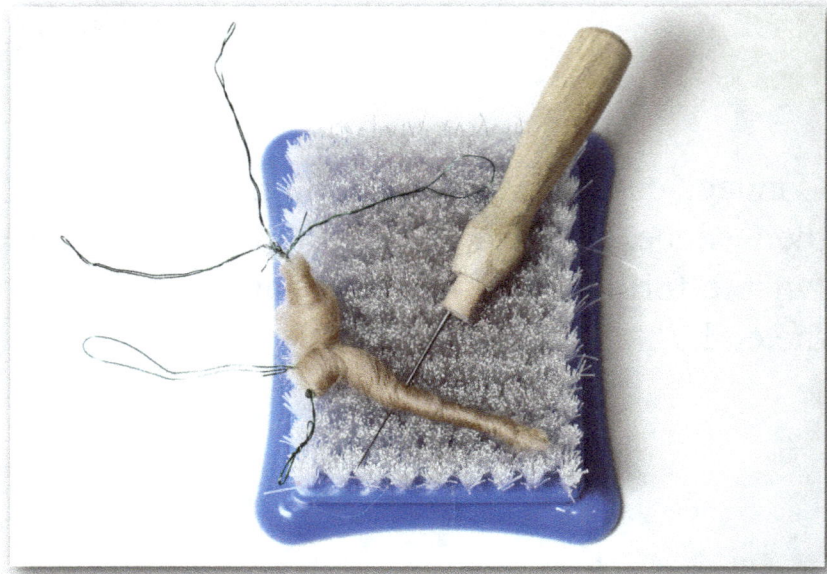

7

Wrap the other leg in the same way, starting from the loop and ending at the dog's body.

8

Wrap all limbs, tail, and neck with the head, and pierce them with a needle to secure the fibers.

9

Add wool for volume on the body and pierce it with a needle until the wool is completely felted.

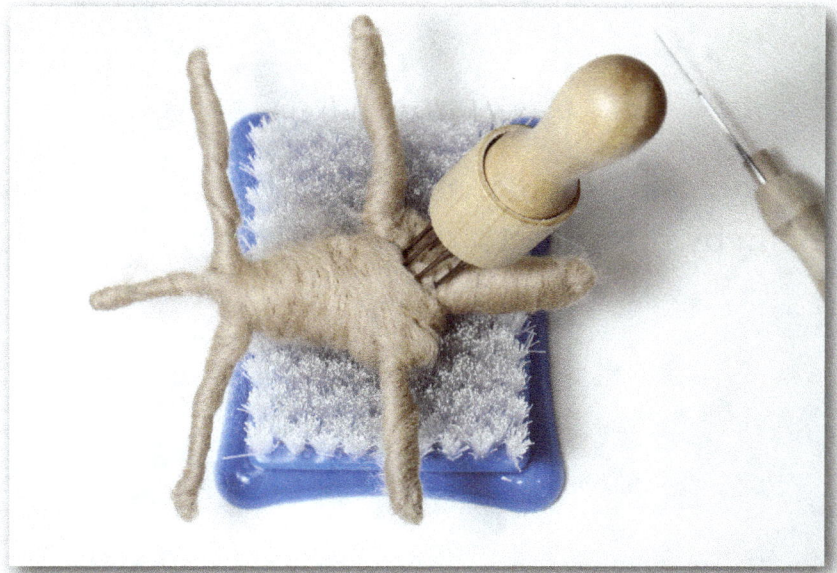

10

Add wool in portions, shaping the body and legs.

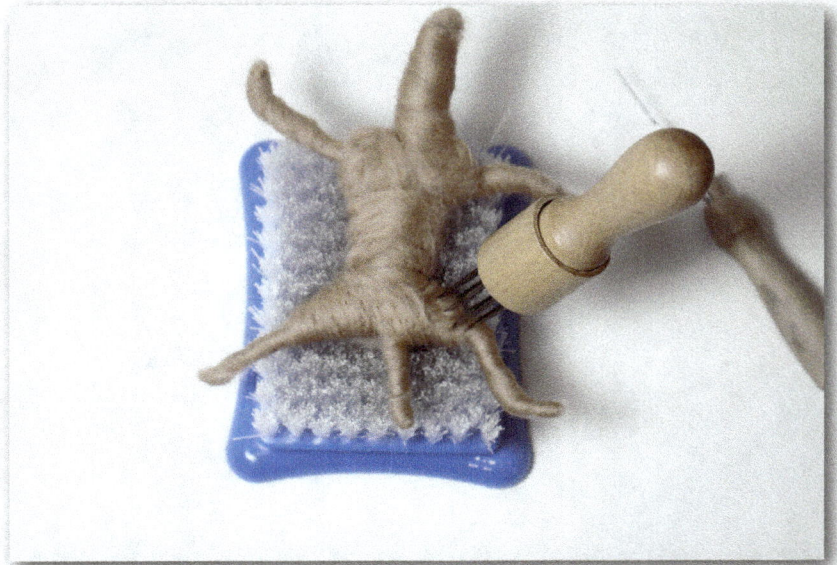

11

Pierce the pieces with a thin needle to secure the wool.

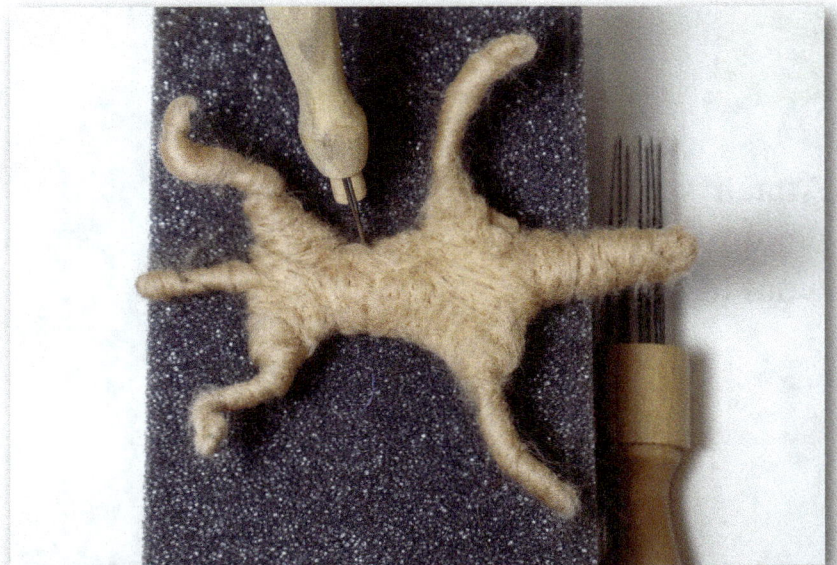

12

Fold the piece in half and secure it again by piercing it with needles.

13

Felt the wool for the ears and attach it to the head.

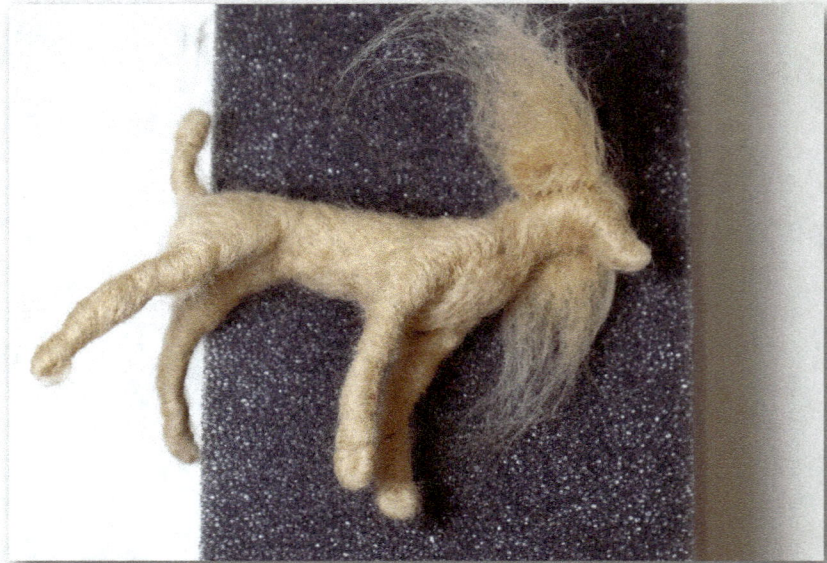

14

Attach several strands of brown wool to form the eyes and black wool to form the nose.

15

The base of the dog is ready. Now you need to work on the fur, giving it the right look according to the breed of dog. In this example, it is a poodle.

16

To make the wool curly, wind the fibers onto toothpicks and moisten them with water.

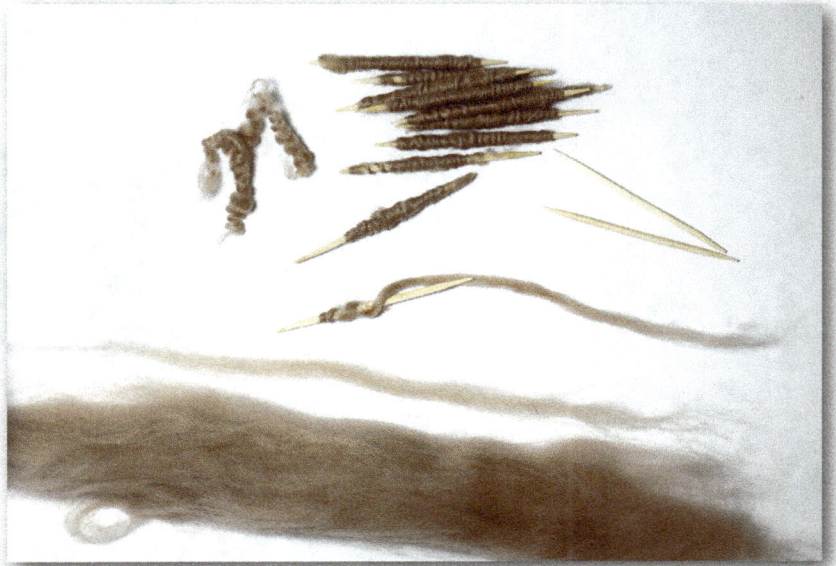

17

After they dry, take off the fibers, rub them together, and attach them onto the dog's body.

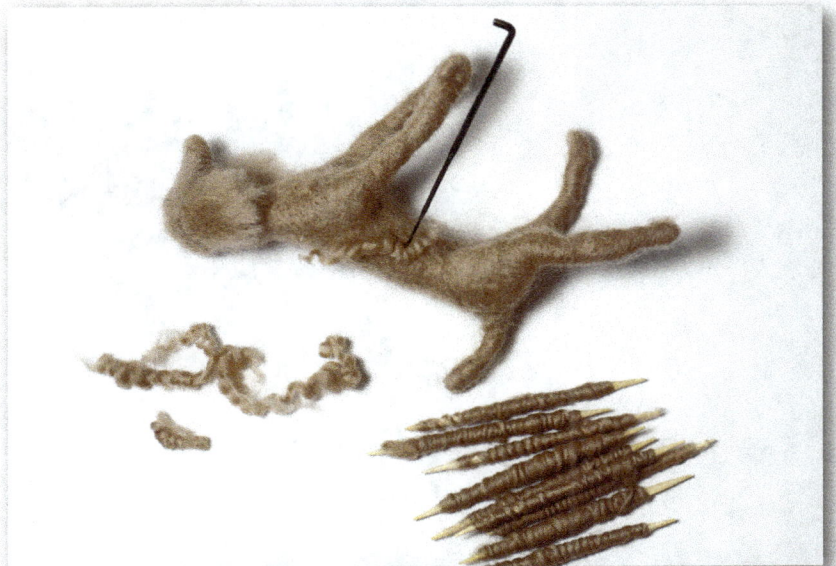

Add wool to the tail, paws, and the head. Your handsome poodle is done.

14. Wire-Based Doll

1

To make this doll, you will need:
- needles of various thicknesses;
- a brush, a pad;
- beige or cream-colored wool, brown wool for the hair;
- 0.4 mm (about 0.015 in) craft wire;
- scissors.

2

Cut two pieces of wire, each 40 cm (about 15.7 in) long, and one piece 60 cm (about 23.6 in) long. Roll one 40 cm piece into a ring and twist the ends together vertically, about 5 mm (about 0.19 in) long; this will be the head and neck.

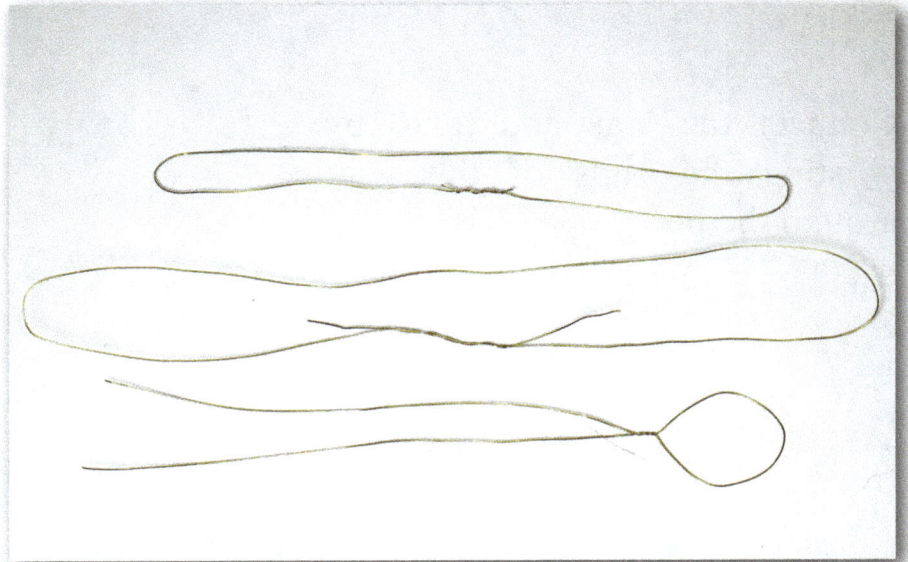

Twist the ends of the second 40 cm piece horizontally; these will be the arms. For the legs, twist the 60 cm piece in the same way, but adjust the length so that it is 4 cm (about 1.57 in) longer than the arms.

3

Twist the pieces for the arms and legs so that loops remain at the ends for the palms and feet. Insert the arms between the ends of the wire under the neck and twist the wire to the end of the torso. The length of the legs and torso with the head should be the same.

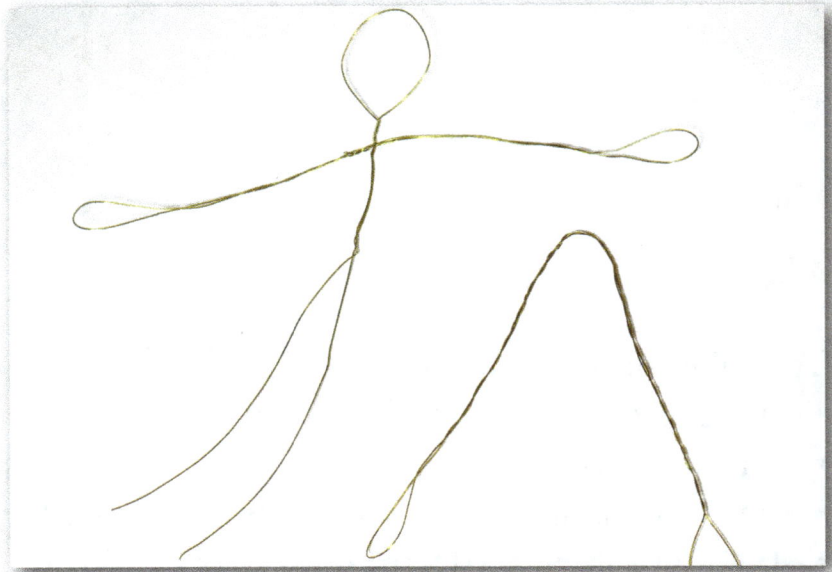

4

Connect the legs and torso by twisting the ends of the wire around the body.

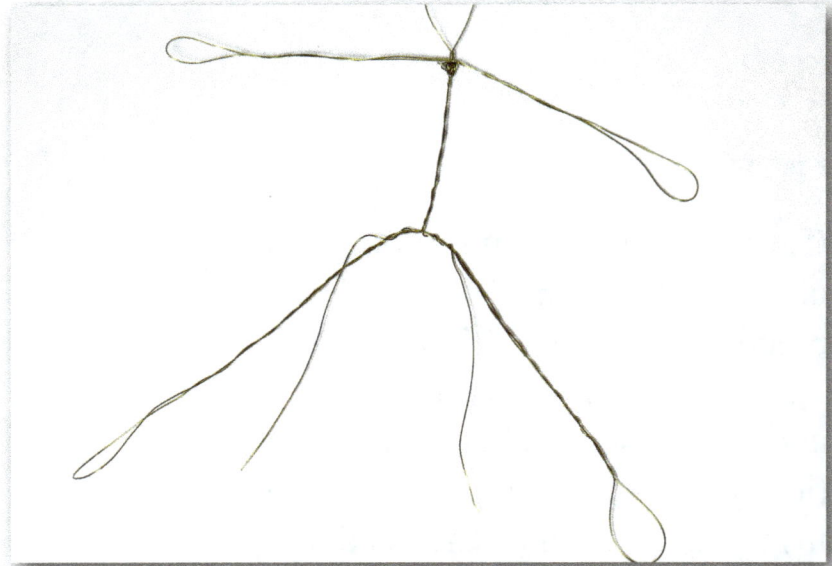

5

Secure the doll's frame again by wrapping the hands around the neck and the ends of the legs around the torso.

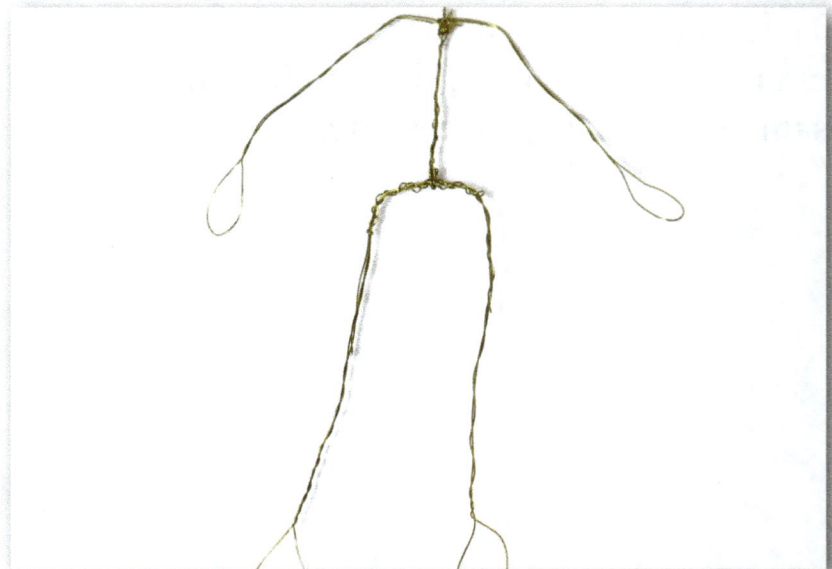

6

Take a strand of wool and wrap it around the wire head first, then place it on the brush, and pierce it with a needle. Be careful not to hit the wire so as not to break the needle. Wrap the head with a large piece of wool and pierce it (placed on the brush). Continue adding wool until you get a ball.

7

Wrap a strand of wool around the loop on the palms, then wrap the wool around the entire arm. Pierce with the needle shallowly, carefully securing the wool around the wire. Do the same with the other arm.

8

Wrap the wool around the loop on the doll's leg to form the foot and then the entire leg. Cover the head with an even layer of wool, like a scarf on all sides, and tie a strand of wool around the neck. Secure it on the neck by piercing it with a needle.

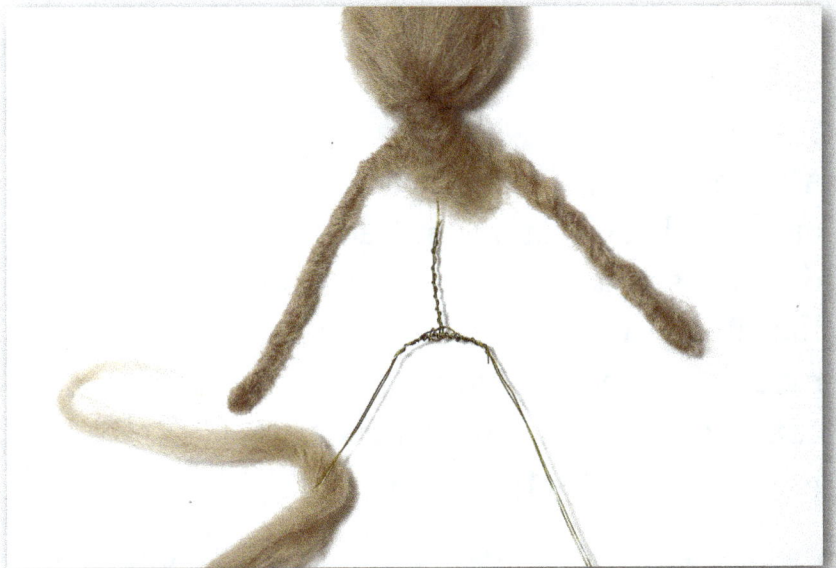

9

Carefully, without making deep punctures, pierce the wool on the arms and legs, placed on a brush or pad.

10

Then wrap the torso with wool. Pierce it with a needle, placed on the brush, adding wool until you get a sturdy doll shape.

11

You can wrap wool around the arms and legs again and add the desired shapes to the body from the back and front by stuffing pieces of wool. If you want, you can achieve anatomical similarity to the human body.

12

Take a strand of hair and smooth it out.

13

Place it on the head from back to front and pierce it with a thin needle along the contour of the doll's face.

14

Attach it to the back of the head by piercing it.

15

Pull the hair back from the face and smooth it down on the head.

16

Style the hair however you like, in a braid or a bun, or curl it. You can decorate it with flowers, a crown, or make a hat, depending on your chosen look.

17

For slippers, felt two flat pieces, placed on the brush, with a multi-needle holder, pressing down on both sides, but not too hard, so that you can stretch and bend the wool around the foot.

18

Place the piece on the back of the foot and secure it by piercing it. Fold the edges of the front of the foot with a needle and pierce them, creating the shape of the slippers.

19

The doll is ready, all that remains is to make clothes for her.

15. Wet-Felted Doll Dress

1

To make a dress for a doll, learn the technique of wet felting wool.

Make a template for the future dress by tracing the outline of the doll on paper. Add a little extra around the edges and cut it out.
2 cm ≈ 0,8 in.

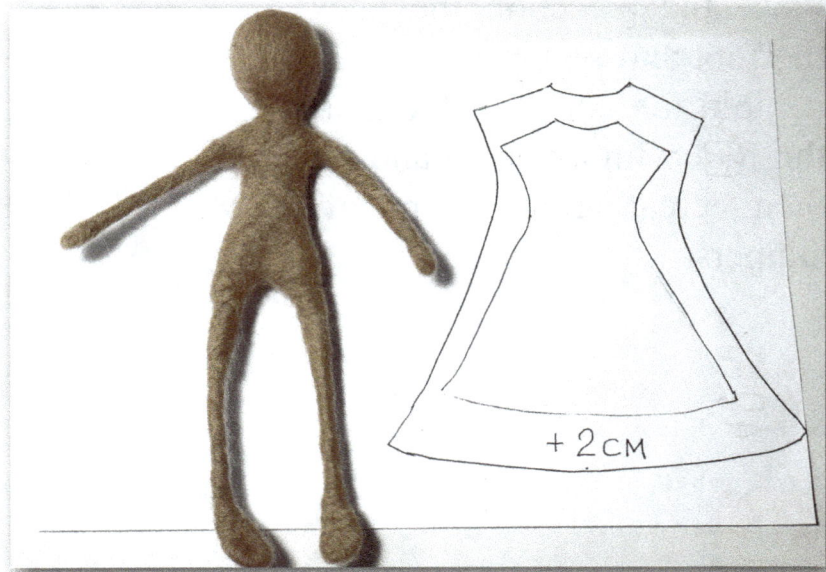

2

You will need:
- a waterproof mat (bubble wrap is commonly used);
- soap;
- warm water in a bowl;
- mesh (e.g., mosquito net);
- a towel;
- a sponge;
- a rolling pin or washboard;
- felting wool of any color;
- decorations for your future product (optional).

3

Lay out the bubble wrap with the bubbles facing up. Place the dress pattern underneath it. Now take the wool for felting. Holding it with one hand, pull small tufts out of the strip. Lay the tufts parallel to each other, covering the pattern.

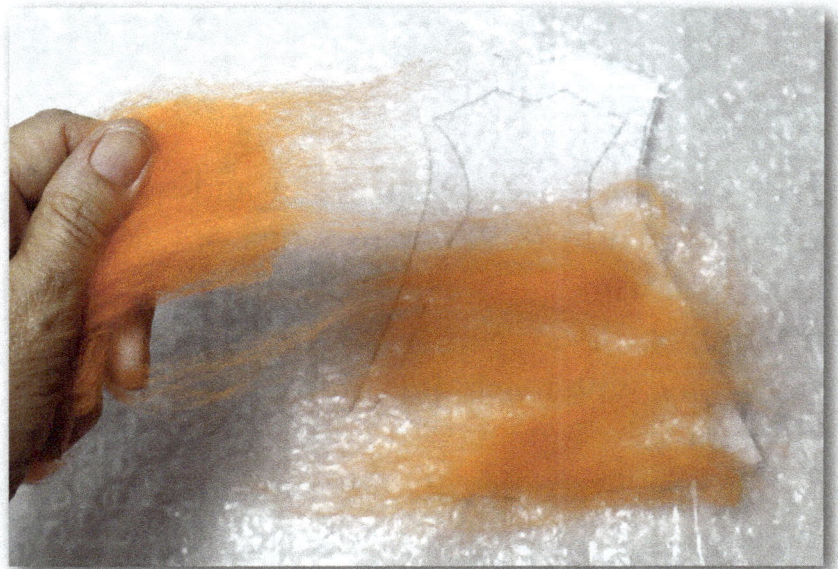

4

Once you have covered the entire area of the template, start working on the second layer. Lay the second layer perpendicular to the first. Carefully press down on the wool and check for any gaps. Gaps are preliminary holes in the fabric. If there are any gaps, cover them with tufts of wool. In this example, the yellow wool was added at the bottom for decoration.

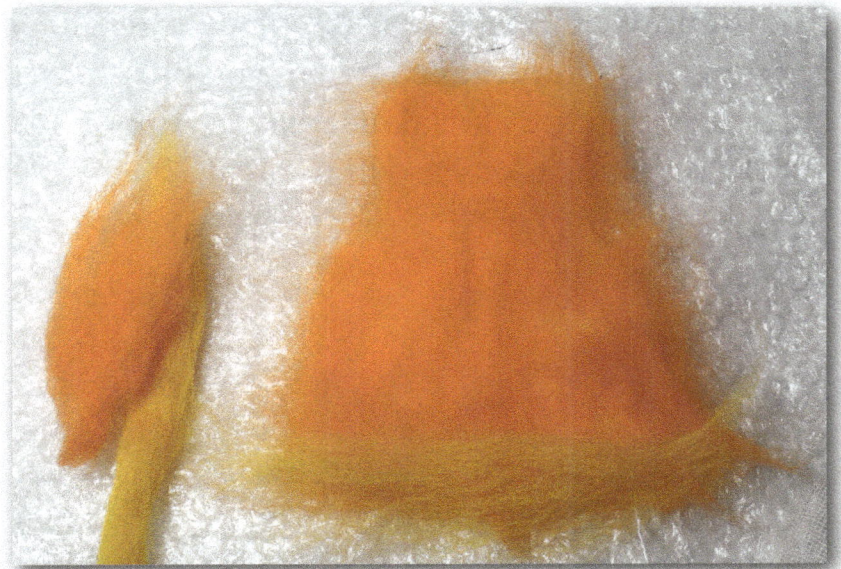

→

5

Take two glasses of warm water and dissolve two to three tablespoons of liquid soap in the water. Lather the solution with a sponge. Cover the workpiece with mesh. It should cover it completely and be even larger than it. Starting from the middle, moisten the surface with the soap solution. To ensure that the solution penetrates deeply, press the piece with your hands. How can you tell if the piece is sufficiently moistened? It should be quite wet, but no water should appear when you press it with your fingers. If water appears, blot the surface with a towel. Balance is very important here: wool that is too dry will not felt, and wool that is too wet will unravel.

6

Put on gloves and smooth out the wool with light circular movements. There should be a lot of foam. Do not press too hard. After a while, check to see if the piece is sticking to the mesh. If so, reduce the pressure.

7

When the front side felts, start working on the wrong side. Turn the piece over together with the mesh, cover it with another mesh, and continue felting the other side.

8

When the other side is ready, take the piece in your hands and rub it with your hands. The first stage of felting is complete. Now take the rolling pin, carefully remove the mesh from the piece, place the piece between pieces of bubble wrap, and roll it onto the rolling pin.

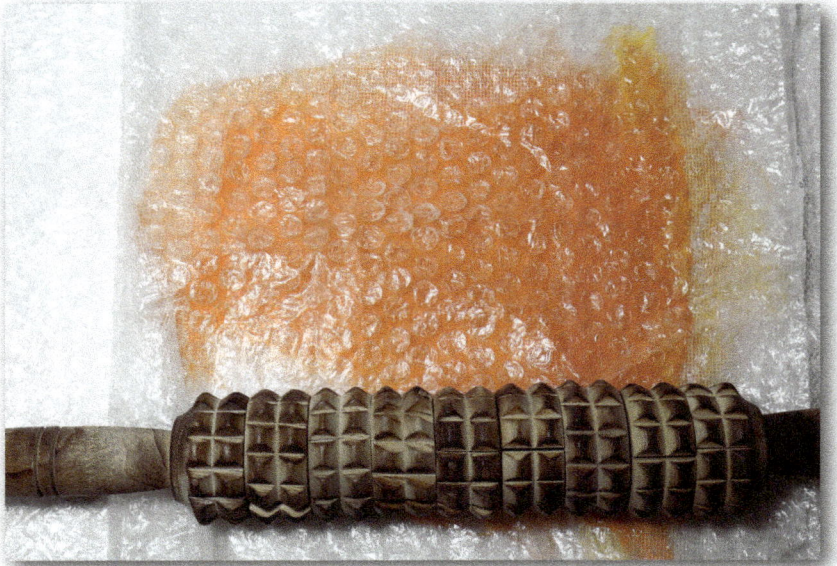

9

Roll the piece across the table; if it slips, place a towel underneath it. Then unroll it, turn the piece 90 degrees, and repeat. If you don't have a rolling pin, you can roll out the piece on a washboard. To do this, spread the piece out on the board and rub it as if you were washing it. When it wrinkles, smooth it out, turn it at a right angle, and rub it again.

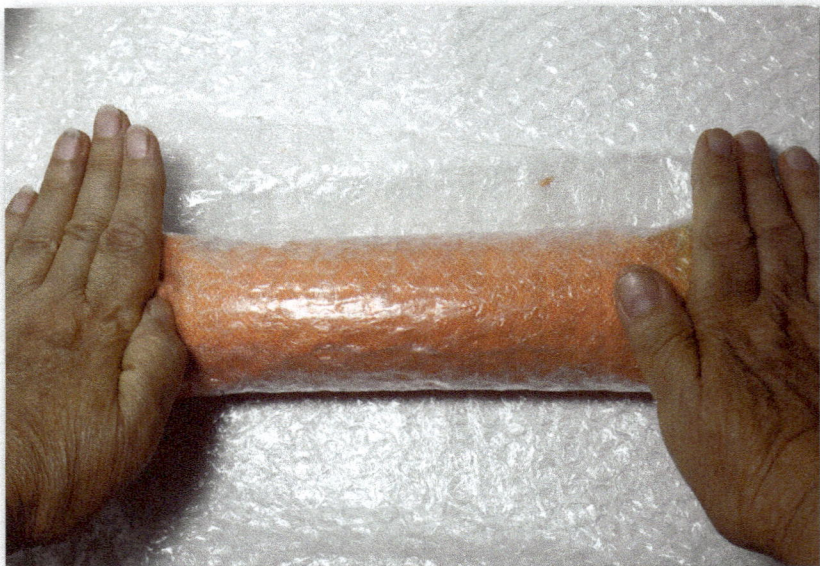

10

Make the second part of the dress this way.

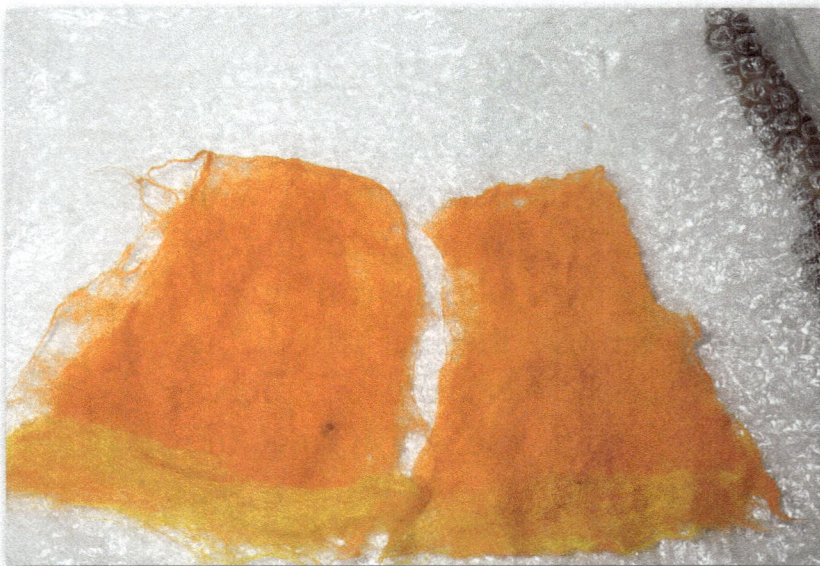

11

Both pieces can be joined together by felting them along the side seams. Place the edges on top of each other and rub them together with your hands, adding soap to make them slide. If they come apart, you can then fasten them together with needles when they get dry.

88

Now that the dress has felted, it needs to be rinsed. Place it in the sink or bathtub and pour hot water over it. Rinse it until the water runs clear.

12

Then rinse it with cold water and dry it by rolling it up in a towel. Then lay it out on a horizontal surface to dry completely.

13

You can dry the dress with a hair dryer. Trim the dress details with scissors, and cut the neckline and armholes according to the template.

14

Secure the side seams by piercing the dry wool from the inside with needles.

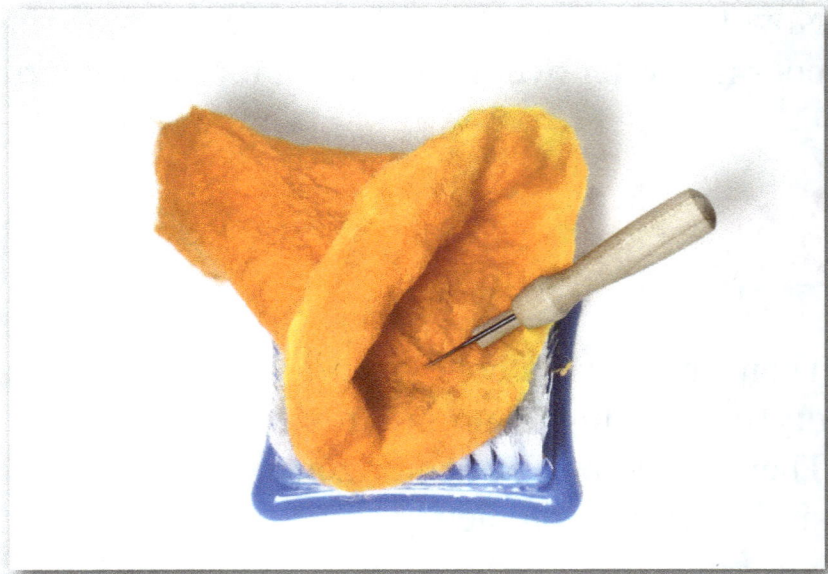

15

To make it easier to put the dress on, join the shoulder seams when the dress is already on the doll.

16

Use thin strands of wool of a different color to decorate the neckline and armholes, piercing them with a thin needle.

17

Tie the dress with a woolen belt and secure it by piercing it with a needle.

18

Decorate the dress as you wish. Create the look of a princess, a fairy, or Snow White by adding various accessories.
The doll is done!

All Videos (Playlist)

or use the link:

cutt.ly/Ur04Att7

For any questions, comments or suggestions, email us at:
kostyayaroshenkocat@gmail.com

I hope you have gained experience and pleasure in felting wool and can now make any product you desire and imagine. I wish you creative success!

Margarita Sidorenko

EASY RECORDER LESSONS for Kids

VIDEO AND AUDIO

60 Songs

First Book Step by Step

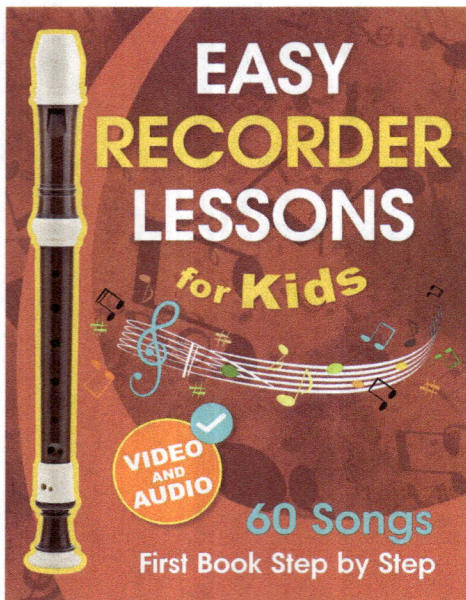

- Learning step by step: starting with more simple tunes, then gradually moving to more complex songs.
- Includes music theory, instrument history, practice, recommendations and many entertaining songs.
- Learn the position of the body and hands, how to breathe properly and play easily.
- Letters above each note and simple explanations;
- Convenient large U.S. Letter print size.
- Video accompaniment to all lessons by direct link inside the book.
- 2-in-1 Book: Recorder lessons and video + 60 Songs.

And it's great for adults

ISBN: 979-8386419004

ASIN: B0BXMX7ZVN

United States   **United Kingdom**   **Canada**

EASY ORIGAMI for Kids and Teens

First Book Step by Step

50 Models

Margarita Sidorenko

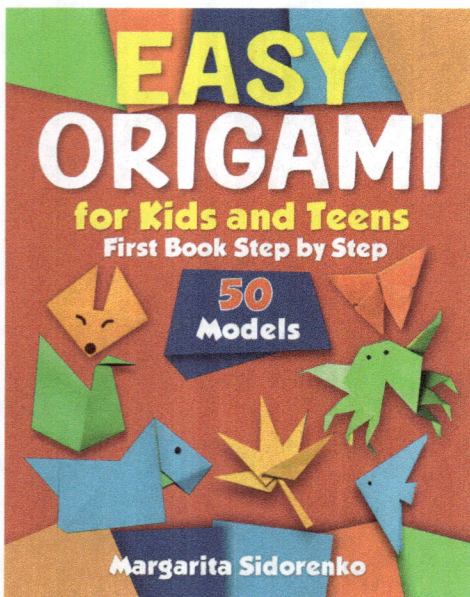

- 35 Easy origami models for kids and teens of all ages.
- Step by Step: at the beginning the most simple models, gradually increasing the level.
- Simple and clear instructions.
- Classic and modern models.
- Step-by-step photos along with symbols and comments.
- Free additional 15 origami models.
- Free 50 Video with a slow demonstration of how easy it is to fold origami.

And it's great for adults

ISBN: 979-8842659029

ASIN: B0B7QFYWFL

United States   **United Kingdom**   **Canada**

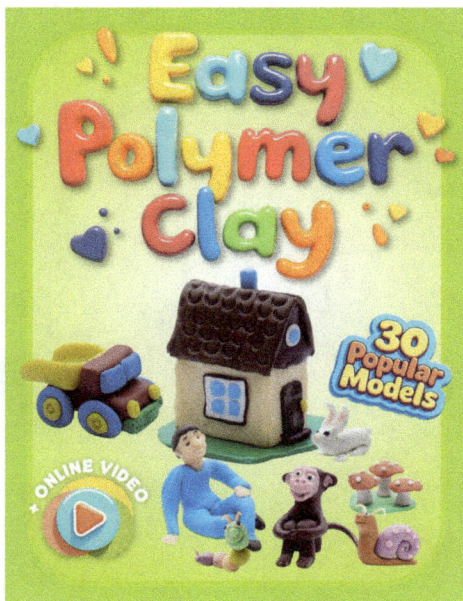

- You can find information about polymer clay, tools and basic instructions for beginners.
- 30 different popular models: a house, a cat, a pizza, a leaf print and more.
- Description and photo of every step.
- Color book, large print and U.S. letter format.
- Additionally, you can watch online instructions on how to make every model.
- Videos are available online and you can download them.

And it's great for adults

ISBN: 978-1962612173

ASIN: 1962612171

United States	United Kingdom	Canada

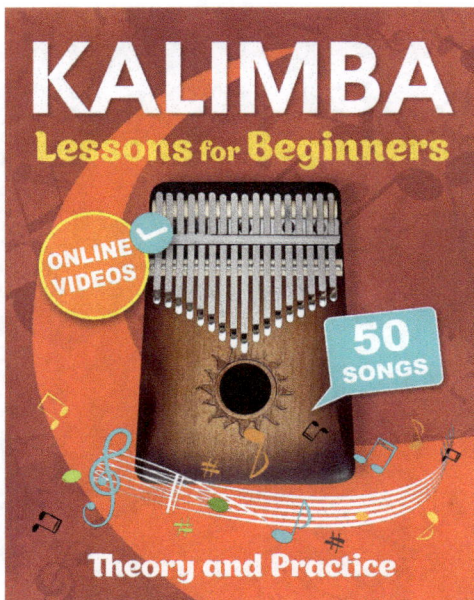

- Step-by-step instruction for beginners of all ages and proficiency levels.
- All the basic theory you need, without the non-essential information.
- A fast and fun way to learn to play the kalimba.
- Online videos with examples for better understanding.
- Convenient large U.S. Letter print size.
- A 2-in-1 book: Kalimba lessons and videos + 50 Songs with sheet music that includes notation.

ISBN: 978-1962612012

ASIN: 1962612015

United States	United Kingdom	Canada

www.ingramcontent.com/pod-product-compliance
Lightning Source LLC
LaVergne TN
LVHW081348060426
835508LV00017B/1470